By the author of:

"How to Live Large on a Small Planet"

"11:11– Inside the Doorway"

"EL•AN•RA: The Healing of Orion"

"The Legend of Altazar"

and

"Invoking Your Celestial Guardians"

The Star-Borne:

A Remembrance For The Awakened Ones

BY SOLARA

STAR-BORNE UNLIMITED

Star-Borne Unlimited
6477 Highway 93 South #6511
Whitefish, Montana 59937 USA

First Edition published October 1989
Eighth Edition published March 1999

Illustrations by:
Mimi Kamp &
Marie St. Marie (Sheoekah Amu)
        Ancient Beauty Studio
        PO Box 704
        Mt. Shasta, CA 96067

Typesetting by:
Mitch Gregoire & Elara Zacandra

Book Design by:
Solara

Printed in the United States of America

ISBN# 1-878246-00-3

An Accelerated Path Homeward

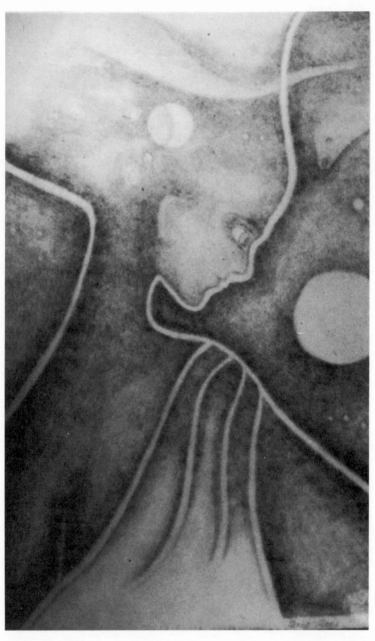

"Facing the Image of Infinity" by Sheoekah Amu (Mary St. Marie)

This book is lovingly dedicated
To the Star-Borne Ones,
To those who remember.

May your commitment be unwavering,
May your courage be strong,
To openly be Yourselves.

Angels walking freely
Upon the Earth,
Journeying Home to the Star.

Introduction
to the Seventh Edition

Six years have passed since I wrote this book. Six years of tremendous change and acceleration. Six years of unprecedented spiritual awakening. When it became time to reprint this Seventh Edition of *The Star-Borne,* I decided to recalibrate this beloved book to better reflect the shift in energies which we have experienced since it was first published.

This recalibration has proved to be quite a journey in itself. I began by rereading this book with red pen in hand. At first, I cleaned up the writing, smoothing out some of the more awkward passages in the text. I even found a few errors which had been undiscovered in previous editions. Soon, I realized that a total recalibration was in order; that we had traveled much further in the last six years than we had known. Occasionally new information popped through which has been inserted into the appropriate chapters. And two small chapters were totally deleted when I found that they served no further purpose.

The entire process was like weeding a garden. The first time through, I removed the obvious weeds. Then came the second editing in which I could see more clearly what needed to be recalibrated. Much of this was done during a visit to Hong Kong in April 1995. I sat in my hotel room perched high above the bustle of that busy city and during the early morning hours, diligently combed through *The Star-Borne* with red pen in hand.

What I realized is that this book is an excellent map of our journey from duality to Oneness. It is still relevant to our present situation. And it is still alive and viable, finding new readers each day who write us with great joy at their discovery that they are not alone or crazy, that there are others who understand what they have been undergoing on their journey of reawakening.

I have also discovered that much of this book aids the completion of our passage through duality. It details the steps which will bring us through the Time of Completion. I know this because I have already made this part of the journey. I have left the Template of Duality behind. And when this is done, much of what is written in this book will drop away. When we move into the Template of Oneness and begin to anchor our beings there, we find that everything has changed. All the great beings who have aided our journey through duality begin to disappear from our lives, melting away from our sphere. The great service of ones such as Sanat Kumara & Kuan Yin, Archangels Mikael & Uriel is now complete, for their Higher Purpose is achieved when we graduate from the illusion of duality. Then they too, are freed to move onwards into the New Octave.

It is in the latter part of this book as we enter the section called *The Homeward Journey*, that I was most curious as to how my previous vision would stand up in the light of what has now been revealed six years later. And I was extremely pleased to discover that it still resonates with truth and is often, stunningly accurate. Especially in the chapters on the Seventh Star which still fill me with excitement and cause my cells to tingle. At the time I wrote this material, I didn't fully understand what I was writing although it felt to be true. Now with our continuing passage through the Doorway of the 11:11, I see with enhanced clarity the accuracy of what was revealed.

Once we journey into the New Octave of the Greater Reality we discover that we are traveling on an entirely new map. Nothing is the same as it was before. Nothing is found in its previous location. Absolutely everything is different and infinitely vaster. Here, we are truly traveling deep into the Unknown. We embark on the most exciting journey ever attempted, into the vast realms of the Invisible. To travel into the Invisible, we must learn to see with new eyes and to follow our hearts as never before. For the foundation of the New Matrix of Oneness is Love. Love like we have never experienced or imagined. Purest, True Love that weaves us all together into the One Heart.

As you know, I am an intrepid explorer into the Unknown. Everything that I have written about, I have experienced firsthand. And I have traveled far enough and deep enough, to know that this journey is real. The processes within this book really work; they will help you to move from duality to Oneness if that is what you seek. This is what has happened to me. And this book, *The Star-Borne*, is lovingly given to you that you also may find empowerment, wisdom and freedom. That you may anchor your beings in the One Heart and be filled with All Encompassing Love. That you may birth your Greater Selves and step into a new future that is bright and true. For by birthing our Greater Selves and by merging into the One Heart, we also birth the Greater Reality.

TABLE OF CONTENTS

THE STAR-BORNE

THE ANGELS

THE STARS

THE HOMEWARD JOURNEY

In The Beginning
There Was
But One Star,
The Star That We Are,
Shining Across
An Empty Universe.

Then it exploded,
Sending fragments of star
Throughout the Celestial Void,
The sky filled with pinpoints of Light,
Thus myriad stars were born.

Maybe you remember now
When we were pieces of star
Spiraling and cascading
In Heaven's vastness.

For remember we must
In order to reunite.
Star families gathering together
To make the journey homeward,
Merging once again
Into the Star That We Are.

Come with me, my beloved ones
And we shall remember . . .

The Star-Borne

The Star-Borne

By now, you know who you are. You are everywhere, thoroughly mixed into humanity, walking among us.

You are found in all walks of life, in myriad occupations and lifestyles, belonging to cultures as diverse as this planet has to offer. Yet, you have not felt that you belonged here at all. Many of you have felt abandoned, as if you had been put up for adoption by your real parents and left with a strange, alien family. When you were young, perhaps you looked closely into the eyes of your mother, father and siblings and wondered who they were and why you were living with them. Gazing up at the starry sky, you cried out for your true people to rescue you from this unfamiliar reality. *Yes, you are one of the Star-Borne.*

When you were a child, you had many unusual dreams and experiences. You tried to share them with your family, but they were often put down as the workings of an over-active imagination. Some of you remember hovering above your bed at night, gazing upon your sleeping body with curious detachment. Or perhaps you experienced the sensation of becoming so vast that it stretched your mind past its limits of understanding. Just when you began to adjust your parameters to being so huge—in a flash you became small, so terribly tiny that it was inconceivable to imagine.

Possibly you felt motion speed up until everything was a blur, making you feel dizzy and sick. Then, without warning, time slowed down to the slowest crawl, driving you crazy with impatience. These experiences of childhood, some which remain with you today, were journeys through various realms of consciousness and multi-dimensional doorways which you were more open to experience when you were young and unschooled in the ways of this contemporary world, where such things are thought to not exist.

You might have seen fairies in the wild places of nature who shared with you their secrets with a welcome joy. For fairies are ever pleased when humans acknowledge their presence and play with them. Indeed, that is how it was ever meant to be. Perhaps Angels came to you at night when you were safely sheltered in the privacy of your room where the world could not intrude. They sang to you the Songs of Stars, ever watching over you, sometimes healing you from illness or despair. Or late at night warmly snuggled in your bed, you were visited by brightly colored spheres of light that were strangely reassuring. *Yes, you are one of the Star-Borne.*

Maybe you felt as if you were lost, that perhaps you had taken a wrong turn somewhere on your journey, ending up by accident on planet Earth. But alas, you cannot remember the way to return home. You look up into the night sky, hoping that the flickering of your dim memories of so long ago will catch a spark and reignite. Walking about this planet in a state of dazed resignation, you know that as long as you find yourself here, there must be some reason. That perhaps, there is some form of service you can render in order to earn your passage home. *Yes, you are one of the Star-Borne.*

But then again, you might be on Earth because you feel that you are being punished for some serious transgression you did *somewhere else*. Possibly, you may remember misusing your power in another world. And now you are placed on this planet in order to atone for past misdeeds. Of course, you have made sure to keep yourself as diminished as possible so that you will never need to face the challenge of being an instrument of power again! You are the ones who are the *walking wounded*—full of swords and implanted devices that you, yourselves, have placed within your own beings. The constant hurt keeps you small and safe from the danger of becoming too strong. Walking upon this planet with a self-effacing shuffle, as if stooped under the immense burden of guilt that you carry. Knowing that you are *unworthy* of being home, accepting the pain of banishment and disgrace without question. *Yes, you are one of the Star-Borne.*

Each of us who is Star-Borne has carried these feelings within us, embedded deep within our cellular memory banks. We have wondered why we are here, why we are so different from the *others*, why we don't fit in with the life patterns deemed *normal*. It's as if we hear a separate anthem than most people. One that touches us deeply, yet, few others seem to hear. And it is the fragments of this precious song that enable us to continue on, as if seeking to put together pieces of an obscure puzzle, sacred to us, yet unnoticed by most.

We gather our reawakened memories as if pearls strung together on a cord, endeavoring to recreate our necklace of remembrance.

Thus it has been as we have lived out our countless incarnations on planet Earth. Sometimes we have so disguised ourselves as to almost pass as normal, experiencing brief moments of fitting in. Though in the end, we didn't feel good inside while acting out our deceptions. Often this literally made us sick, sometimes so ill that we even died. Always returning to yet another embodiment, a chance to try again.

Then there were our inner rules and codes of conduct. These often conflicted with those which prevailed on Earth at the time. We seemed to be born with different rules, values and laws to abide by. Actions that were perfectly acceptable for everyone else were harmful to us, while we were able to do things that were not permitted most of humanity. This not only proved quite confusing, but frequently got us into a lot of trouble. A state of affairs which has continued into the present day.

Sometimes we were blessed by meeting another who seemed to understand—maybe they also heard the sacred song. What a gift when we could share our feelings, communicating to each other our most precious and private yearnings. For those brief moments we didn't feel so lost and alone. Often we would receive a penetrating look from the eyes of a stranger which would lift our spirits, giving us hope that *somewhere* there were others who understood.

But most of the time we were painfully alone and unacknowledged. And still we searched. Still we cried out to the stars to come and carry us home!

Even physically we were different. When we were sick, our temperatures often went down instead of up; we frequently had low blood pressure and clogged sinuses. Our spines were sometimes strange. We could bend our bodies in unusual ways, what they call *double jointed.* But it was in our eyes where we most stood out. We had a look about us or a way of perception that was definitely different from most. We could *See.* This means that we could see beyond what is normally perceived with the physical eyes. We could look into the Essence of another, reading their soul, their thoughts and innermost feelings. This made many uncomfortable around us. In fact, often we were disliked and ostracized due to people's fears of being seen. It wasn't as if we were trying to see more; we just could, without any effort at all. *It is simply part of being a Star-Borne.*

Thus we lived our lives—alone, separate, lonely and misunderstood. Ever seeking for fuller understanding of our plight. Always searching for the key which would return us home. Finding solace whenever we could—in a flash of friendship, the fleeting passion of love or through communion with Nature.

The beauty of Nature gently nourished us, soothing our restlessness, grounding us with her enduring patterns of change—the cycle of birth, death and renewal.

Here, alone with nature, we almost felt home on this planet. Its simplicity embraced us like a mother her child. She nourished and protected us from our immense vulnerability. We could relax for a moment, breathe openly and deeply, while gathering strength for our return to the world.

The world assaulted us from the beginning, no matter what time period or geographical location where we incarnated, although some cultures were more enlightened than others and some embodiments easier. We tried shielding ourselves with all kinds of armor to mask our deep sensitivity. Of course, this never gave us any real protection. Finally, the combined weight of multiple layers of armor proved to be an unbearable burden. We could barely move, yet continued feeling far too exposed.

Throughout time, we have been thrust into all the

diversity of expression inherent on Earth. We experienced being rich and poor, wise and ignorant, powerful and downtrodden. Ultimately, it all became a blur. *We had seen and experienced everything.* It seemed as if there was no more to do. All ancient peoples and races of man had become our own people. We had known intimately all foreign lands as our homeland. We had spoken many tongues, done all kinds of labor from kingship to serfdom, been male and female, young and old, over and over again.

We began to experience a profound sense of weariness from our extended cycle of lifetimes on this planet. Often to see another beautiful sunset or to hear yet another rooster crowing to announce the dawn would move us to silent tears of deep fatigue. How many more times would these things repeat themselves?

We had done everything, been everyone, too many times. Joy and sadness blurred together in endless repetition.

Yet, there was still something which had not been experienced by us. This was the one thing for which we had ever searched and yearned. It was the act of remembrance which we knew was absolutely necessary in order to find the key which would enable us to return Home. Yes, that which was most precious, had ever eluded us, in spite of all our earthly adventures. . .

Go within, go deeply within
For you are being restructured.
The changes are deep
They are thorough,
They are everlasting.

You mourn the death
Of the little one,
Of the ancient one,
Of that which you have known
Since your first Earth birth—
The sweet personality self
Whose outspoken ego
Carried you through
Countless adventures.

For that little one
Truly falls away
As separate and distinct,
As self important.
It merges inside you
Into that conglomerate
Known as your Angelic Self.

Angel name is merely
Star lineage name.
No individual personality.
Filled with limitless Love
Yet so extremely detached.
It is as if you aren't here,
But You truly are.

In your new form of
Angelic fragment of Star,
You cry for what is gone,
Yet want it no longer.
But what shall fill the gap
Between what is past
And what is to come?
The most important question,
"Who am I?"

I know the many things
That I am not.
My freedom from them comes
Simply because I have experienced
So much for so long,
That I am everything.
I am the One; I am the Many.

Not being simply this nor that,
I am everyone, everywhere.
It is difficult to separate
One voice, one identity,
One thing that really matters,
From the new vastness
Which I have become.

Alas, poor small self
Sitting abandoned by the wayside,
Savoring your fading memories,
Yearning for attachment
And ego's control.
Old dreams drifting steadily
Out of sight on distant horizon
Like last summer's faded sunsets.

Come inside, forgotten little one,
For there is room for all,
I am the Many, you see,
Come and play with me.
You'll find that love abounds
Embraced by our Angelic wings
Enfolding us in sweetest bliss,
In Love, we become the One.

Yet know not I
Whom I might be.
Where comes this authority,
This knowingness,
This vast beingness,
This sense of wholeness?

Am I already fragment of Star,
Personality no more,
Merged into physical body
Yet much larger still
That I can fill the sky
Just by breathing and expanding
Into all that I truly am.

For not only do I ride and glide
Upon the undulating star waves,
I merge into them as well.
I am the planets,
I am the stars,
Radiating, pulsating,
Worlds within worlds.

I am a dimensional doorway,
I am a Pillar of Light,
A beam of the Great Central Sun.
In my wholeness, I am One.

Duality

There came a time when we had traveled the roads of third dimensional spirituality as far as they could go.

We had obediently done the prayers, rituals and practices that were supposed to enlighten us. We had committed ourselves to being on a spiritual path. Yet something was admittedly missing. We still weren't happy or fulfilled or home. Everyday life ever presented a formidable challenge to us. Sure we were fine, as long as we were meditating or being alone. We loved going *out there* to the spiritual realms. But we didn't always appreciate the shift back into worldly, secular life.

We found ourselves split between two realities—our spiritual and our physical worlds.

It was often difficult shifting between the two realities as it shocked our sensitivities to move abruptly from one world to the next, each being so different from the other. In either world, we felt incomplete because we had to leave part of ourselves behind in order to enter the chosen reality. Thus we continued to separate ourselves in two. Often, this was expressed as a division in the flow of energy through our chakras or energy centers. The upper chakras belonged to the spiritual realms while the lower chakras represented our physical, human world. We experienced great difficulty in getting our energy flow to unite the upper and lower energy centers. We resided in the upper chakras when we were being *spiritual* and in the lower chakras when we had to deal with the world. *No wonder we weren't feeling whole!*

This situation caused great distress and conflict within our emotional body. As our emotions became increasingly out of balance, we began to judge them as not being *spiritual* and tried to isolate and cut them off. If we experienced anger or sorrow, we felt that we were off our spiritual path. Our poor human selves were deemed unacceptable and unworthy for entrance into the higher realms. Thus we continued to close off and deny very real portions of ourselves simply because we did not know how to integrate the spiritual with the human.

Our poor divided selves suffered and languished in the sea of duality while we searched for the key that would make us whole. . .

The Awakening

The awakening did not take place overnight. Actually, it had been happening all along. Only we did not realize it.

Remember that we had been gathering and stringing our pearls of remembrance since the beginning. And eventually, we began to perceive a change. First, we started to honor our uniqueness. We embraced the fact that we were different and learned to enjoy our sense of aloneness.

As we accepted being alone, we discovered that we need not be lonely. In our solitude we learned to enter the mysterious realms of deep silence. Here we found the key to many new worlds of revelation.

The silence proved to be one of our greatest teachers.

It embraced us, wrapping us in a profound sense of contentment and peace. We were initiated into new dimensional levels of awareness which had previously been unknown to us. We not only became used to the silence, but found that we required steady doses of it to maintain our inner equilibrium and connection to Source. It became one of our truest allies.

Next we started working on self-love. This proved to be one of the most formidable tasks of all, for long had we been locked into guilt and denial, feeling unworthy of love and happiness, or else we would not have found ourselves on this planet at all. We would have been home where we belonged, where we had always yearned to be. Thus we have had to learn to relinquish our sense of punishment and abandonment.

Instead of constantly pouring out love to others as a distraction to avoid facing our own internal turmoil, we had to learn to love ourselves.

Turning our attention to nourishing and honoring ourselves without guilt, without feeling we were being selfish, was a major challenge.

We were so afraid of being judged harshly by others as egocentric or spoiled, that usually we just did what people told us to do, or thought what they told us to think, instead of listening and honoring our inner voice. And of course, this caused more self-judgement, making it ever more difficult to love ourselves. But with the passing of time and much effort on our part, we finally began to accept ourselves. Gradually, we started to genuinely like ourselves.

Self acceptance was so tremendously liberating that it became increasingly easier to respect and express our true feelings and insights. And surprisingly enough, the more aligned we were to our Highest Truth, the more we lived and walked our Truth—the less criticism did we encounter. Not only were we beginning to feel good about ourselves, but others seemed to appreciate us more too!

It's funny how long we held fast to the judgement that it was dangerous to openly be ourselves on this planet. And now we are finally discovering that it is the only safe way to be. That's why we should use extreme caution when making any kind of assumptions. It's important to remember that all assumptions are based on only a fragment of Truth. Let's stay open until more of the whole picture is revealed.

Our next project had to do with the issue of power. One of the ways in which this manifested was in the battle between the sexes for supremacy and control.

Long ago, women on this planet were given great power and authority. Instead of serving wisely, they tended to use men as their slaves, regarding them as vastly inferior. Great abuses of power were done by women in those distant times. Some legends, such as those of the Amazons, speak of those days. Even today, there are a few tribal societies hidden away in the remote corners of Earth where women still rule in a heavy handed manner. Eventually, women's power was taken away.

Next, we entered an era where men were given the authority. We are experiencing the end of this phase right now. One might think that those who had suffered terribly as victims, experiencing firsthand the results of misrule and abuse of power would have developed the compassion to rule wisely. Unfortunately, this has not been the case as observed in earthly history.

When men seized the reins of power, they proved themselves to be just as bad as the women had been. It was now women's turn to become second class citizens. This condition of inequality is still prevalent in many areas of the world, although the situation is steadily changing to one of greater balance and harmony.

Finally, as the tides turned once again, women began to reawaken and reclaim their lost identities while confusion reigned. Women looked to men as their role models for power. In their haste to emerge, they started acting like men, equating men's behavior with empowerment.

Of course, this was not the case, and women have had to learn to be true women, not some silly stereotype, but the real thing. In order to be an empowered woman, each of them has had to embrace and accept the full scope of femininity. This includes the female *shadow side* which is admittedly scary.

The shadow side of women could be perceived as the dark witch Goddess immersed in magic, manipulation and heartless seduction—not exactly the image which most women want to identify with. Yet this shadow side is ever present in a most threatening, subtle way within all women until they learn to integrate and make peace with it. And it has to be acknowledged and embraced in order to experience wholeness.

To achieve this, the shadow is loved into wholeness and her qualities are integrated and transformed. These are insight instead of intrigue, intuition replacing manipulation, and the emergence of woman's deep healing wisdom. Thus are women coming into their true feminine power.

Men have undergone a similar journey. While they thought that they held the power, they were living under an illusion, because there was no balance. Their power was of the aggressive type of dominance, not a rule motivated by wisdom and service. Besides, just as they had disempowered women, they had also shut down their own feminine sides. This served them not, for who remained on Earth to provide the clear insight and devoted nurturing that the feminine brings?

As the balance of power, or rather the imbalance of power, was in the process of shifting, men began to open themselves up to their inner female. Opening the doors to their emotions, they activated their receptivity, intuition, tenderness and sensitivity. You might think that this would balance everything out, but it did not.

Now we were beginning to have strong women who had claimed their power in a balanced fashion, and lots of sensitive men. What we didn't have were strong men and they were greatly needed!

Thus men were forced to go one step further and reclaim their true male identity. Believe me, they were no more thrilled about this than the women had been, for they too, had to accept and unite with their terrible shadow side. Talk about frightening! The male shadow is the ruthless warrior, bloodthirsty and cruel; definitely not someone whom a sensitive male wants to claim as his own. Yet, it simply had to be done.

And whether it was out of desperation or great courage, men in ever growing numbers have been undergoing this process of integration with their male shadows. They are discovering the deep springs of strength, fidelity and vigorous capability which the male shadow brings when he is loved into wholeness.

And now comes the happy beginning for men and women on planet Earth because they can finally come together in the way it was always meant to be—as equals, complements and co-creators.

We have waited such a long time for this to manifest. What a blessing that we are finally ready for this level of completion and balance.

But of course, the process of reawakening is endless. There is always more to be achieved. Although we had begun to make peace with our male / female issues of power, it was now time for us to stop seeing ourselves as helpless victims of forces beyond our control. No longer were we weak, little children being meekly tossed about by the twists and turns of fate. We were beginning to grow up and take responsibility for our own lives. Thus we began to transcend karma and step off the wheel of cause and effect. This required a profound shift in our awareness, moving from a patterning of duality to that of Oneness. And although we strove mightily to transform, our old patterns exerted such a strong hold over us that often our progress was slow and arduous like swimming against the prevailing current.

This entailed an endless cycle of letting go, releasing and surrendering—followed by a phase of stubbornly holding on to what we knew so well, our old habits of control and denial. It seemed as if we could never surrender enough.

We were always called upon to release more. At first, we resolved to let go of the old habits which had gotten us into much trouble in times past. But always were we aked to release more. Now we needed to surrender some of the aspects which we liked about ourselves, the glamourous garments of the ego, which had served us well in times past, even releasing some of our hard sought ancient knowledge and personal power. *Ultimately, we were asked to let go of everything!* What a supreme challenge we faced, surrendering all our previous security and values. What a battle we fought!

Ah, the doubts and fears that we encountered along our path to reawaken. Our rational mind held sway like a crusty tyrant, fighting for its very survival, testing us with numerous doubts at every turn. But what if we were going crazy? What if this search was leading nowhere? Telling us that we must be practical and rationalize every step along the way. Weighing ourselves down with the endless possibilities of failure. Tying us up in knots like gossamer threads of spider webs, rendering us powerless to be our True Selves.

Often we believed these doubts and fears to be real, giving them life and power over us, thereby keeping ourselves imprisoned in illusion as we cried out to be reborn anew.

It was like the mighty elephant being plagued by a tiny mosquito who captures so much of the elephant's attention, that the elephant forgets who he is, so immersed is he in the ongoing struggle.

As we continued to steadily awaken, we discovered that our beings were shifting from a horizontal pattern to a vertical one. On the old horizontal path we gained our knowledge second hand from teachers, books and other people's experience. We believed things because others said so and since we were so unempowered, we didn't expect to find out for ourselves.

Horizontal patterning is the road of duality—full of manipulation, control and innuendo. It can be very subtle and insidious, for nothing is out in the open or directly experienced. It is the realm of second hand rumors, wherein no one ever expresses their true feelings. Everything is layered under the ambiguity of what *someone else* said or did. Talk about giving away your power! Some highly skilled practitioners of the horizontal path are still among us, so watch for them. And don't fall for it.

Increasingly, as our awakening progresses, we are shifting our consciousness to a vertical path. This is the realm of direct experience, receiving our own guidance and knowing straight from the One.

This is how everything was learned back at the beginning of each earthly cycle. This is how the great visionaries, mystics, saints, plus the founders of all the world religions, received their Higher Truths. What is truly amazing is that it's so easily available to all of us!

Of course, there is a challenge connected with being tuned into your own direct hot line to the One which is trusting what you receive. Learning to listen to your own inner voice and then to act upon it; beginning to live your life as an embodiment of what you know and believe. It may sound easy, but often it is not. We have been conditioned to worry about what other people are going to think of us. How are they going to react if we speak our Truth? Well, how are you going to be true to yourself if you don't?

As we continued on, there were always glimmers of hope and true vision along the path. Enough to carry us forward with an ever increasing sense of knowing, for our clarity was returning at last. We were beginning to feel lighter. Our weariness was dropping away. Although we still experienced doubts and fears, we recognized them for what they were.

While still bound by the illusion of separation, now we knew it to be an illusion. We had gained a toe-hold in the Greater Reality.

And nothing was going to shake us loose, for we had labored too long to give up the struggle now. Gradually, our sense of struggle diminished, as we transformed with increasing ease!

The next thing that happened had to do with our physical bodies. These poor bodies had been constantly abused and denigrated by us. Most of the time we had thought of them as our prisons instead of our temples. You could say that we went through life with our suitcases packed, since we knew *or hoped* that we would soon be leaving the planet. Then in a flash of revelation, we discovered *to our overwhelming dismay* that *in order to go home, we would first have to fully enter the human body!*

This meant that we needed to restructure and

enliven our physical forms so they could serve as empowered instruments of the Higher energies we had courted for so long. What a shock this was to us—an unwelcome surprise to many. A whole new level of work opened up.

Now we had to put our attention into the bodies which we had long neglected. We could no longer separate spirit from matter. Indeed, our task was becoming clear, we were to serve in the process of uniting Heaven and Earth, moving from duality into Oneness. First, we had to achieve this Sacred Union within ourselves!

I Am Solaris Antari:

Now you begin to understand,
The shift is taking place,
The effects of restructurization
Are becoming apparent,
You are being reborn.

This multi-dimensional awareness
Is simply the embodiment
Of your Angelic Presence
Merged within third density form,
Union of Heaven and Earth.

Reawakened and reunited
You step forward
Into that which you always have been,
As the discarded remnants
Of old fears and limitations
Dissolve and disappear.

You have stepped through the doorway
Of dimensions four and five
Which anchor & merge deeply
Within your physical body.

This change is thorough,
It has long been awaited, yearned,
And prepared for arduously.
There is no more going backwards
Into narrow modes of consciousness
Where old doubts and fears dwell.

Your cells have been restructured,
Your pre-encoded memories reawakened,
You have received reactivation
And are hereby empowered
To be the vast being you truly are.

The scope of this is far greater
Than anything you can yet imagine
For truly can it be stated
That you are the One;
You are the Many.

There shall be no more separation
As the illusion of duality drops away
With the entrance of integration,
The recognition of the inherent Oneness
That permeates everything, everywhere.

Arise now, my beloved brethren,
And know that you are all
As Golden rays of the One Star.
Brilliant beams of Light
Each radiating purest love
From the heart of the One.

The time of concepts is past.
Release them gently.
Let the Winds of Change
Dance among you
For you are finally free.

Know that Heaven and Earth
Reside within you,
Wedded in Sacred Union
Like night and day,
Always at play.

Feel the joyous limitlessness
Of your vast starry being
So happy to be enlivened,
Experiencing the ecstatic union
Of opposites within you.

This is what you have yearned for.
It shall be denied no longer.
You are free to swim in the sea of completion
Containing your sweetest unfulfilled desires
As Divine nectar fills the cup of bliss.

The more you bring Yourself into your body,
The Lighter you shall become,
As heaviness and fatigue melt away,
Ancient memories dim and fade,
And the final residue of Karma
Dwindles into nothingness.

Reborn Ones,
Listen to our Song,
Surrender into flight
Across both Earth and sky,
The Golden Dawn has come!

Restructurization

Thus began the profound process of restructurization.

What this meant was that we had to facilitate and achieve a massive inner transformation right down to the basic levels of our DNA codings. We needed to realign our physical vehicles to be receptors of the accelerated light frequencies now streaming into the planet. We had to prepare for the entrance of our radiant Light Bodies, for the sacred merger that was soon to come. We were being called to serve as Pillars of Light and anchors of the new Divine Dispensation. All of this affected our pre-encoded cellular memory banks which were hereby activated.

Each of us contains within ourselves pre-encoded patterns designed to activate when our conscious awareness reaches certain levels of awakening.

These pre-encoded memories were implanted within us before our first earthly incarnation, to be activated by various triggers under a time release mechanism. This is happening right now.

Many of you have undoubtedly been experiencing some unusual physical symptoms for the past few years.

Among these are periods of immense sluggishness when you seem to have little physical energy. Often this is because you are working intensely on inner levels of your being and most of your energy is occupied with the process of restructurization and integration.

At times you may develop strange eating habits where you want to eat only one type of food or have cravings for something that is not normally considered healthy. In matters of nourishment, I find that it is best to follow my inner promptings, as weird as they may occasionally seem. Many of us are now discovering that we need far less food than before and are being drawn to lighter and healthier foods.

Other symptoms of restructurization are a loud, constant ringing in the ears, pains in the back of the neck and sacrum, and a rapid vibratory rate. You may experience shortness of breath and an erratic heart beat. Instead of constantly running to doctors who often find nothing wrong, if you feel that your condition needs attention, you might seek out a wholistic healer with very clean energy who can better understand what you are going through. But then again, *always* follow your intuition, because you *may* need to see a medical doctor. It's important to remain open to all forms of help.

From my own experiences, I know that we are undergoing tremendous changes right down to our basic cellular structure, and that it is natural that we often feel we are dying, because much of us is.

Appropriately enough, one of our strongest triggers for change has been sent to us from On High by what we shall term, the long, Golden Trumpets. They have already issued *the Call to Reawaken and Remember.* Followed by *the Call to Action.* Next shall come *the Call to Return.* And we are indeed, remembering. Emerging at long last, from our slumber of what has seemed like countless aeons.

We have been greatly aided and activated by the presence of other Star-Borne ones—those who remember, members of our Angelic, Starry Brethren. For like flowers in a field, we all blossom at different times. *Thus are we reawakening one by one, hundreds by hundreds, thousands by thousands, until all of the Star-Borne are fully activated and empowered.*

As each of us reawakens, we add our voice to the resonance of our song, which is the Song of One.

This Song becomes ever stronger until the vibrations of its Celestial Resonance sing out throughout the planet Earth, birthing it anew. Then we shall discover that we are serving our sacred Purpose by melding spirit into matter, transforming everything into radiant Love. And thus, my dear ones, do we receive our ticket Home. Of course, by then the illusion of separation will have totally dissolved, and it will not matter anymore, for we shall be Home wherever we find ourselves to be.

Inside Mount Shasta

Deep within Mount Shasta, there is movement. I can feel it within my entire being as a profoundly unsettling energy, which finally causes me to stop all outer activities and look within. Immediately I can see large, egg shaped objects called starseeds, which are in the midst of being transported. These are similar in appearance to the objects in the film, *Cocoon*, except they do not contain beings and seem to serve a different purpose. The starseeds are being tended by an ancient root race that dwells deep inside the sacred mountain.

Somehow, I am strongly connected with these starseeds and whenever there is activity involving them, I am affected. Today they are being moved from one area of the mountain to another. This is to facilitate their further development. They are being transported deeper inside for the duration of the winter months. As the starseeds enter these warmer chambers, closer to the volcanic fires, certain protective coverings are being removed. I experience this change as disturbing, since I am closely linked with these starseeds. I am told that I originate from the same substance.

There are several of us in the Mt. Shasta area who have this connection. It's as if we are attached to the starseeds by some sort of umbilical cord. We feel intimately whatever they are experiencing. Our breath gives them breath, our eyes give them sight, etc. As we perform this function in the world for them, they also serve us.

They are our connection to our origin. They are that part of us which lies in embryonic suspension within the dimensional doorway known as Mt. Shasta. It is the part of us as true multi-dimensional beings which awaits birth. Each of us who feels this connection has a personal starseed deep within the mountain, ever being tended by those of the ancient root race.

These ancient ones entered inside the mountain long ago after having completed their phase of service upon the surface of the planet. Perhaps, they are the ancient Lemurians spoken of in tales of old. The care of these starseeds represents their final cycle of service to planet Earth. When it is completed, they will be released forevermore. This shall be affected by the total germination of our starseeds and by our transmutation of matter and gravity as we develop our crystal, Light Bodies.

In order for the ancient root race to depart when their time arrives, they must merge together, compressing themselves tightly under great external pressure, until they form one small pinpoint of crystalline Light. This Light shall then collapse into itself causing an implosion whereby a doorway will be created into the dimensional universe of their origin.

I am told to please remember that none of this can take place until our starseeds have been birthed, for the ancient ones are bound to complete their chosen task. I perceive these beings as rather lumpy looking. They are weary and call out to us to continue our process of reawakening. They sing to us while tending the starseeds in the most ancient of tongues.

Books by Solara

- [ ] How to Live Large on a Small Planet...... $15.95
- [ ] The Star-Borne $14.95
- [ ] 11:11 - Inside the Doorway $15.95
- [ ] EL*AN*RA - The Healing of Orion $14.95
- [ ] The Legend of Altazar $12.95
- [ ] Invoking your Celestial Guardians........ $10.00

Meditation Tapes by Solara

- [ ] The Starry Council........... $10.00
- [ ] Temple Invisible $10.00
- [ ] True Love/One Heart $10.00
- [ ] Unifying the Polarities $10.00
- [ ] Voyage on the Celestial Barge $10.00
- [ ] Archangel Mikael Empowerment......... $10.00
- [ ] Star Alignments $10.00
- [ ] Remembering Your Story $10.00
- [ ] The Star That We Are $10.00
- [ ] The Angel You Truly Are $10.00

Music Tapes by Solara & Etherium

- [ ] The Lotus of True Love $10.00
- [ ] Through the Doorway $10.00

The Sacred Dance Series

- [ ] The Earth-Star Dance $10.00
- [ ] The Sacred Spiral Dance $10.00
- [ ] The Greater Central Sun Dance $10.00
- [ ] The Starry Processional........... $10.00

Live Starry Songs

- [ ] The Tahitian Star-Borne Reunion......... $10.00
- [ ] The Second Gate • Ecuador $10.00
- [ ] The Australian Star-Borne Reunion...... $10.00

- [ ] Please send me more information and add me to your mailing list.

To Order: Please include full payment in check or money order *(US funds on US bank only)*. Add postage of $4.00 for first item, 50¢ for each additional item in US, Canada & Mexico. Overseas orders sent airmail $7.00 plus $1.00 each additional item.

Name: _____

Address: _____

City: _____ State: _____

Postal ZIP Code: _____

Country: _____

Phone: _____

FAX: _____

email: _____

Starry Name: _____

Total Cost of items ordered: _____

Donation: _____

Shipping: _____

Total Enclosed: _____

Mail To:

Star-Borne Unlimited
111 Glen Lake Drive
Eureka, Montana 59917 U.S.A.

phone • (406) 889-5288
fax • (406) 889-5255
email • solara@nvisible.com

Visit our vast website!
http://www.nvisible.com

IMA TA GO WAY LA
KA-RO KA-RO MO TE MA KA-RO
KA-NA GO WAY LA GO MA LA
HRN . . . HRN . . . HRN . . .

This last sound reminds me of heavy machinery.
(Only once before have I heard otherworldly sounds like
this, made by Hopi Katchinas during their Homecoming
Dance, *Niman Katchina,* at Old Oraibi, Arizona.) The
ancient ones move slowly amongst the deep pools of
molten fire, carefully turning the egg-shaped starseeds
to keep them warm and balanced.

Soon I discover that there are others who live
within the mountain. I begin to see them clearly now.
They are wondrous beings of Light! They direct the
activities here and encourage the ancient ones, giving
them the strength to finish their final Purpose.

These Light Beings communicate directly with me
and others like me, guiding us through the process of
transformation. They are the ones who brought me to
Mt. Shasta and oversee all activities connected with the
starseeds.

As part of my preparation, they bring me to their
sacred chambers within the mountain. Here I am placed
on a pallet and tended to, aiding and accelerating my
process of restructurization. As I lie upon the pallet, the
chamber transforms itself into a crystal pyramid. The
Music of the Spheres fills the deep Silence. The Masters
of Light surround me quietly, emanating an intense
radiation of Love. Love which is all pervasive, which
dances through the air like crystalline rainbows.

As the Light Beings raise their hands above me, I
feel an envelope of warmth and protection surround me.
They begin to chant, HO, HO, HU, *(for my lower
chakras,)* then EE, EE, A, *(for the middle ones)* finally,
AH, AH, WA, *(for the upper ones).* The sounds realign

my molecules as my vibratory structure responds and balances itself into a new harmonic resonance.

I open my eyes and see a Golden Light extending from my belly. This is the umbilicus which connects me to my starseed. Another Golden Light streams forth from the top of my head. This is where my Angelic Presence enters. Then I notice my Golden Angel, *who is me*, standing close by my head. I feel extremely blessed by its radiant Golden Presence. As I arise, I look deeply at my Angel whose eyes penetrate my very soul. I feel the activation within my being of great reservoirs of Love which open up and begin to flow through me.

My Angel gently touches my forehead. Now I can *See* with utmost clarity and calm wisdom. Now I know. I truly remember. I look back to my arrival upon this planet long ago. Did I not arrive in my starseed? The memories reawaken, flooding my being with a tremendous sense of excitement. I know that my starseed and I share the same blood, but it is not the red blood of humans; it is liquid, crystalline Light filled with tiny Golden stars. It filters back and forth between us through the Golden umbilicus.

I am told that from this starseed many Angels shall rise into the Light of Remembrance, and that I too, must tend it with Love and devotion. The fruits of this shall be many. From this effort, Earth shall be filled with Angelic song, singing as if with One Voice. And the Mother shall know youth and innocence once again.

Two years later, I was told that I had successfully completed my merger with my starseed and was free to leave Mount Shasta. And perhaps the ancient ones have finished their final service and returned Home.

The Sacred Pause

Before we journey further, we ask you to join with us in what we call, *The Sacred Pause.*

This is the moment when we stand before the open doorway which we have sought for so long. Our passage through this doorway is certain. The time of hindrance is past. In this sacred moment, we shall pause and look backward at the vast distance we have traveled to arrive at the open portal which now awaits.

As you look behind you, you can see with pristine clarity the long journey you have taken. View with heightened perception your struggles and sufferings, as well as the immense pain and joy that you experienced.

With a profound sense of loving compassion, bless everything that you have experienced, knowing that it has served you well by bringing you to the threshold of this doorway.

Look carefully at the people whom you encountered along the way. Remember the ones who served as your lovers, your teachers, and most especially, the ones who stood in your way, trying to block your progress. Although you perceived these ones as adversaries at the time, now look again. You will see that they served you the most. What great teachers these supposed enemies were, pushing your buttons until change was provoked, forcing you to grow stronger in order to survive, constantly pressuring you to develop compassionate understanding.

Remember also those whom you loved, some of whom openly loved you; others did not. Ah, the trail of broken hearts that each of us has traversed. Opening our hearts in loving trust, only to be let down time and time again. Vowing never to love again, but, of course, earthly vows are ever made to be broken. We opened our hearts repeatedly, sometimes finding a measure of solace in a relationship which felt ordained by Heaven. These calm seas of love manifest spurred us onward, for by merging our Essences we had touched too deeply to forget. We were given a taste of the sacred union of souls which we had constantly yearned for in the very fibers and cells of our beings.

Of course, there were times when we ravaged and destroyed the hearts which others so freely offered to us. We could display great cruelty and coldness and often did. We did not always play the part of victims, you know. Many times—noble, gentle hearts, magnificent missions, even lives, were painfully, yet eagerly, sacrificed on the altar of love. We have acted out all the roles in Love's grand theatre. And what purpose did this wild drama serve?

It is that old issue of balance in order to become full and complete. Each relationship that we experienced served as a mirror for us, perfect mirrors of either what we were or

what we were not. Often these were painful mirrors because they forced us to grow and change.

By expanding into areas which we had neglected within our own beings, we grew stronger and more whole. Our relationships pointed out to us, in an often excruciating fashion, parts of ourselves which we had locked away in a state of denial, that we refused to own as belonging to us. When presented with such a mirror, we experienced an instant revulsion as well as a compelling attraction. Learning at last that the harder we tried to hold on to our partner, the further away did they go. And when they tried to cage us, we escaped either by flight, spiritless resignation or death. That's what happens when you cling to someone out of the lack within yourself. Such was the paradox of relationships.

What drew us into partnership again and again was our enduring quest toward union and wholeness. We felt that total union could only be achieved outside of ourselves, if we could just find the perfect person. And we spent much time searching for the mate who would heal us and make us complete. If only the Gods were sufficiently merciful to let us find our true love! A relentless, never-ending search which can only end in disappointment or enlightened freedom.

Sooner or later, *and it was usually later for us,* we began to realize that true union takes place within. And that looking for what we desired outside of ourselves was an exercise in futility. As we turned our attention within, we found what we had been looking for all along. It was that easy, only it took us so long! The funny part is that once you make the inner union between the male and female polarities of yourself, this actually facilitates the arrival of the perfect outer partner, if you want one.

So you see that each of your chosen partners, *and*

you did choose each other, throughout your long cycle of embodiments helped bring you into wholeness. No matter how the relationships appeared on the outside, whether they were happy or sad, unrequited or fulfilled, they served you greatly. So please send a shaft of forgiveness, profound gratitude and love to all those who helped you along your journey to reawaken.

Perhaps you now realize that although you often judged yourself to be making mistakes, that in truth, no mistakes were ever made. Your cycle of embodiments was perfect—a symphony of balance containing all the needed elements to create your unique song. The wrong turns were always correct; they provided the fuel for your growth.

Now that you remember who you are, possibly you wonder how you could have forgotten for such a long time. Why was it such an arduous struggle to reawaken? Why did you have to experience the constant pain and suffering of the deep sleep of ignorance for so long? Surely this could have been circumvented. Maybe you did fall from grace?

Please, dear ones, see that total immersion into the full sphere of third density was an absolute necessity in order to achieve your goal. If you had descended into matter with your memories intact, would you truly have developed the necessary compassion and understanding for the rest of humanity? Or would you have judged them as inferior and not worth the bother? Scan your memories back to the time of Atlantis and you will see an example of this. For the history of Atlantis contains a perfect lesson on the perils of spiritual arrogance which can only lead to the ultimate destruction of all that you hold sacred.

In order to become balanced, we had to be thoroughly humbled and we were, time and time again. For each exalted incarnation, we served in several meek and debasing ones.

However, from the humble ones, we learned our sense of dignity. And from the regal embodiments, we developed our sense of humility. Remember, "We serve by ruling. We rule by serving." Admittedly, it has taken us awhile to balance our many polarities, but it was necessary for us to first experience the full spectrum of dynamic opposites.

As we look back over what has appeared to be aeons of planetary incarnations, we realize that measured by Heavenly Time, our earthspan has been brief, though exceedingly fruitful. Where else could we so fully manifest ourselves as Love in Action? What a glorious opportunity to express the fullness of our Beings through bodies, minds and emotions! We are wedding spirit with matter, creating an alchemical union between formless and form, between the seen and the Unseen. First and foremost, this union has taken place within our very own beings! This by itself, is worth the years of struggle and sleep. And it has all taken place in the flicker of an instant, too brief to deserve more than a notation in the vast chronicles of time.

The Quantum Leap

Before you stands an open doorway.

It is now time to step through . . . . .

This is the process wherein we emerge

As conscious, multi-dimensional beings,

Serving on planet Earth

Fully awakened.

Part One: The Star-Borne

In the Beginning
There was
But one Star,
The Star That We Are.

Together,
Merged as One,
We shimmered and rotated
In the vast empty Heavens.

Each spark,
Each glowing ray,
Was the manifestation
Of our combined Essence.

Our Star
Was one being,
Complete,
Containing everything.

Then . . .
Critical mass.
Our Star
Imploded,
Then exploded
Sending
Starry fragments
Of itself
Shooting
Across
The
Endless
Empty
Universe
Up,
Down,
Under
And through.

Cascading fragments
Cast outwards
Upon Heaven's currents,
Star waves
Churning with
Debris of Star.

Fragments
Split apart

Becoming
Smaller,
Smaller,
Smaller.
Spreading
Throughout
The sky.
Smaller,
Smaller,
Smaller
And ever
Further
Apart.

We held together
As best we could.
Focusing
Our vision
On the One Star
That we had been,
That we truly are.

Smaller,
Smaller,
Smaller
Fragments
Rent apart

In mandalic display
Like fireworks
Illuminating the sky
In their brief
Moment of glory.

Becoming
Further apart . . .
Separate . . .
Remote . . .
Isolated . . .
Alone . . .

Finally,
We could
Become
No smaller.
Thus
We developed
Into individualized
Units of consciousness.

This is termed
The Birth
Of the Angels.

Part Two: The Angels

Possibly
You remember now
Flying so freely
Through the Heavens.

Separate, yes
But limitless,
Still remembering
Our Divine Origin
United as One
Vast Starry Being.

All Encompassing Love
Flowed through us
As we danced and played
With our Angelic Brethren,
All of whom
Were but fragments
Of our One Star.

How could we not love
Those who were but mirrors

Of our Unified Self.
Each of us simply a facet
Of the same shining crystal,
Rays of One radiant Star.

Ah, the games we played
In those Golden Days,
Combining our Essences
Into vast Heavenly Beings,
Filling the silent skies
With waves of song,
Dancing joyously
In shimmering starlight.

And when we merged
The tender Essence of Love
With each other
Making Truest Love,
We sent rippling currents,
Rocking the star waves,
Birthing new galaxies
Spiralling ever outward
Across the celestial seas.

Our transparent Bodies of Light
Sparkled with rainbow tints
As though brushed with stardust
In truth, that they are.
Remember, we are a Star.

Now we were winged
Angelic wings that soared
Outstretched in fullest flight
Gliding effortlessly
Throughout the endless night.

Ah, the glory and the freedom
Of those bygone times,
So joyful and precious
Now that we know
What we chose to undergo.

Maybe now
You remember
As do I.
The memory fills me
With forgotten longing,
Banished tears
Raining down
My weary, worldly face.

Dare I speak of the Call,
That urgent summons to serve.
So many of us responded
And descended down to Earth.

At first, it was child's play,
Angels openly creating on Earth,

Birthing a new Paradise,
Walking about with wings unfurled,
So magnificently huge and Heavenly,
Life on this planet was a delightful adventure.

Then dear ones,
I'll remind you gently,
The Second Call sounded.
The Time of Decision had come.

Most of the Angels departed quickly
Returning to the Celestial Realms,
While all of us
Who hear these words,
We chose to remain and serve.

The task sounded simple.
TRANSMUTE MATTER.
Merge Heaven and Earth.
Transform duality into Oneness.

Naturally, we assumed
This could be completed
Effortlessly and quickly,
But, of course, that was before
We had ever experienced
The illusions of duality,
Time and separation

Part Three: The Fall

Yes, the descent into matter
We remember it well
Although long has it been veiled
Hidden behind the mists of time.

The brightest of us
Volunteered willingly
For earthly service
By receiving that lethal blow
That locked us into the prison
Of density, of forgetting
Who we truly are.

Our experiences of the Fall
Are carried with us today.
Shock, betrayal, abandonment,
Deep sorrow, anger and guilt
Lodged within our cellular memorys
Waiting until now to be released.

We forgot, dear ones,
We truly did.

Forgot our wings,
Forgot our Star,
Forgot our Divine Origin,
Forgot that we are Angels,
Forgot our limitlessness,
Forgot That We Are One.

Thus we judged ourselves severely,
Adding upon ourselves the weight
Of immense guilt and judgement,
For had we not vowed
Never, ever, to forget
The Star that we truly are.

But dearest Angelic Brethren
Please know within your hearts
That this too, was preordained.
Forgetting was but a necessary part
Of the process of transmutation
Of third dimensional matter
That we, ourselves, had chosen to do.

Therefore, judge not yourself harshly.
You have not failed your mission.
Understand this and forgive,
For you must love yourself
That you may be healed and loved.

We of the Heavenly Realms
Who have remained at Home
Cradled in the One Heart
Have utmost love and gratitude for you.
We honor your sacrifice and service,
We understand the reasons why.
You need no longer cry.

Part Four: The Golden Cord

During that timeless instant
That endured forever,
Heralding the onset of separation,
You as an Angel emitted
A stream of Golden Light,
A holographic projection
Of your Self,
Downward, earthward,
A Golden Beam of Star
Stretching all the way into matter.
This was how you descended so far.

A tiny starseed embedded itself
Into the density of Earth,
Sent by shaft of Golden Star.

This seed was the only part of you
Which needed to descend so far.

Above in the starry Heavens,
Stood a huge Golden Angel
Watching over you.
This Angel is truly you,
Only you have long forgotten
That the part of you who incarnated
Was but a tiny fragment
Of the vastness of your Higher Self.

At this moment of the starseeding
Of planet Earth by the Angels,
There was experienced a sensation
Of splitting apart, of division,
Though, in truth, no separation
Ever took place.

The Golden Beam which brought you here
Has constantly remained in position,
A Golden Cord always connecting
You to your Golden, Solar Angel
From whence you were birthed,
To which you shall return,
That who you truly are.

This Golden Cord is really a ray
Of shining Golden Star,

Yes, the Star That We Truly Are!
See, my beloved ones,
That although we have long perceived
Ourselves to be far from Home,
We were never alone,
Or separate or lost.
We never left the One's embrace.
We are Home right now.

This long Golden Cord
Has ever served us
As our link between
Spirit and matter,
Heaven and Earth.

Throughout your cycle of endless embodiments
This Golden Cord has remained intact,
Always connecting the earthly you
To your fully empowered Angelic Self.
Although you have often perceived
Your Golden Angel as being
Outside of you, separate from you,
As a Guardian Angel, perhaps.

This Celestial Guardian has guided you,
Ever protected and inspired you,
Enfolded you in All Encompassing Love,
Understood you even more

Than you have understood yourself,
And judged you not!

Part Five: The Call

Now the Call has sounded once again
Inspiring us to rise up and reawaken,
To shake off the shards of sleep
And remember what we once knew.

The Angels, those shining Golden Ones
Who have watched over us so patiently
Since the birth of time in dawn's creation,
Call out to us with resonating Angelic song
To receive them, to acknowledge their Presence,
And to anchor them inside ourselves
Into the full Light of conscious embodiment.

For to make the transition
From duality to Oneness,
Climbing up the Golden Stairway,
Retracing our footprints back Home,
We must lift ourselves beyond duality,
We must balance and unite the opposites,
Melding all polarities back into One.

Thus your Angel Calls out to you
To enter into your physical vehicle,
Anchoring into your very cells
To surrender your identification
With your clamorous little self.
The ego which served you so well,
By bringing you to this door,
Serves you no more.
Now is the time to allow
Divine Oneness to be your guide.

Never, ever before
Throughout the shifting sands
Of rising and falling history
Have Angels been free to incarnate
Into the Earthly frequencies,
Anchoring themselves
Into the root of matter.

Now this is finally possible
For you have done your work here well,
Dear Servers of Divine Destiny,
By transmuting the density
Into ever higher octaves
Of heightened frequencies of Light
You have hereby entered upon
The Accelerated Path Homeward.

The Angels

"The Prince of Peace is Coming" by Sheoekah Amu (Mary St. Marie).

My Story

This is my story of how I discovered that I am an Angel...

I had the good fortune of being brought up in a conscious, though somewhat eccentric and unbalanced, family. My mother was very aware of the spiritual realms. When I was a young girl, she taught me about the ancient civilizations of Atlantis, Lemuria, Egypt & Assyria. These were familiar places to me. I had no question of their existence.

When I was seven and eight, I was taken to U.F.O. conventions in the California desert where many people openly thought that my mother and I were from the planet Venus. Looking back, I'm not sure why this was; it was just something that happened. I saw many U.F.O.s and fireballs of light during my childhood; this also was an accepted fact. In my young innocence, I simply assumed that this was a common occurrence for everyone. Fairies also, were openly communicated with.

Throughout my entire childhood, I had an active imagination, which was encouraged. Much of the time I played alone with my many imaginary friends. As I reached my teen years, I began a compelling search for the deeper meaning of life. This caused me to explore many different forms of established religions. In spite of my openness, I could never find what I was looking for, nor could I even put it into words. Recently, I found some of my high school poetry in which I wrote that I was an Angelic Being of Light. Little did I know at the time just what this meant.

I began to discover that I had a problem which was being *too strong,* or at least that's what some people told me. I seemed to have too powerful of an energy field even when I was being quiet, for some to be comfortable with. Not wanting to disturb others or make my life any more difficult than it already was, I began to shut myself down so I wouldn't be *too strong.* Yet I wondered why my being carried such a large forcefield of power when there never were any safe outlets where it could be comfortably expressed. I just didn't fit in with the way things were on this planet.

For many of my early years, I really wanted to fit in and be accepted as normal. This finally climaxed in my early twenties after I had gone to ridiculous lengths to be like everyone else and it still didn't work. People always knew that I was different. At long last, by my mid-twenties, I simply accepted that I was not the same as most people on this planet and tried to make the best of what I regarded as a truly terrible joke.

As I grew older, my spiritual search intensified. I delved into astrology, numerology and the *I Ching.* Studying the ancient religions and civilizations of the planet, I felt a deep kinship with many of them. For years I immersed myself into the ancient cultures, even going so far as to study Quechua, the Inca language. Each hidden corner of the planet felt familiar and I had a profound love and kinship for the natural peoples. I began to remember myriad past lives. This was often triggered by meeting individuals with whom I had shared powerful embodiments. By encountering them in the present, the doorways to remembrance were flung open.

For eleven years I had a store, first in London, then Boston & finally, in Taos, New Mexico, in which I sold ancient treasures from all over the world. I began to accumulate a large collection of ethnic music which sang to my soul of remembrance. Had I not been everyone, everywhere? And indeed, when I lived in the mountains of Peru in the early 1970's, I found myself telling the native children their ancient legends which had somehow been forgotten by them and remembered by me!

I was blessed with three remarkable teachers during this period. One was a mysterious man from Turkey, one a Hopi woman chief—Mina Lansa, one a Sioux medicine man—John Fire Lame Deer. Each of them taught me not so much in words, but by their vast beings and by creating situations which challenged me to awaken fast.

One evening many years ago in my private meditations, the Great God Ptah of ancient Egypt appeared carrying numerous implements of power and wisdom—ankhs, orbs, wands & sceptres. Slowly, he ceremonially handed these to me while intoning that my ancient powers were being restored. And indeed, it was so. For now, I seemed to remember much of what I had forgotten. I knew ancient prayers in forgotten tongues, sacred mudras to the sun, remembered how to make myself invisible and how to call forth my dragons for protection. Thus began a most wondrous year. I seemed to have all the answers and many people came into my store to ask me questions. I was accepted by Tibetan Buddhists as one who had undergone many initiations, by Native Americans as one of their own, by Hindus as a Hindu, etc.

But of course, this was just a stage on my path and almost a year later, Ptah reappeared to me. He said that it was now time to lay aside the ancient energies. So with deep gratitude, I set aside those old implements of power which had served me well. Thus began a year of excruciating awkwardness in which I didn't know anything! As people came to ask me questions, I would tell them that I knew nothing. I felt like a baby learning to walk, constantly falling down. It was not a particularly enjoyable year. But somehow I knew that if

I persevered, if I could go past this immensely awkward stage, that something new and exciting awaited.

Then one night I was meditating when suddenly my inner vision opened and I found myself in these great starry caverns. I was told that this was the Great Hall of the Og-Min, the home of a starry brotherhood who existed in a simultaneous dimension. The air was filled with the sounds of low chanting. Banks of white candles burned continuously. I was clad in a long, white, hooded robe. Most wondrously, the caverns were filled with many others, similarly clad, whom I recognized deep in my soul to be my true kin. A deep peacefulness embraced me. I felt Home.

Next a starry being appeared at the front of the main cavern. Holding up his four fingered hands, he began a discourse called *The Crystal Transmission*. I learned many things that evening, though little came in the form of words. Mainly, I experienced a profound reactivation of my cellular memories.

After this experience, I discovered that I could return to the Halls of Og-Min at will, for they existed beyond the confines of time and space. It appeared that I had an earthly self who was living my life down here, while another part of me was ever in attendance in the Halls of Og-Min. They taught me much and I began to write down their teachings as a guide for the deep inner transformations that I was now undergoing.

This opened numerous doors for me into the Unknown. I felt like an explorer sailing off to a new land. It wasn't all fun and easy; in fact, much of my life has been extremely difficult and lonely. During this phase, I had to relinquish the concept of control which was not easy for me. And of course, we are always given the choice of surrendering gracefully or having it bashed out of us. Unfortunately, being a stubborn, willful sort, I usually chose the latter process.

I had been told to be prepared to let go of everything. And while I thought that I was doing this, *with a few qualifications, of course,* I soon discovered that anything that I tried to hold onto, was immediately yanked away from me. And often, what I willingly offered to let go of, would remain. Such is the paradox of surrender!

Up to this point, I had a certain ease in dealing with the material world. Inventing my jobs, I always worked for myself and enjoyed a moderate success. I was an able organizer and producer, had a popular, highly unusual, radio program and still ran my beautiful store. Suddenly all this changed. I began to get sick with unspecified illnesses that neither wholistic nor medical practitioners could heal. But inside, the message was clear, I had to drastically change my life or I was going to die.

So I quit the radio, stopped producing events, sold my house and store and bought a small house composed of four old mining shacks strung together in a row, topped off by a tin roof, located in a remote mountain canyon in Arizona. This was eighty miles from the nearest supermarket and one hundred fifty miles from the closest city. I moved there with my daughter, dog, two birds & five cats with no idea of how I was going to support us or what I was going to do.

On the plus side, the surroundings were beautiful with large oak, sycamore, cedar & walnut trees. A creek ran through the land for much of the year. And for neighbors we had deer, mountain lions, javelinas, coatimundis, bears, rattlesnakes and a profusion of birds. *I might mention here that I'm not the wilderness type, wasn't even the camping type, so this drastic change in lifestyle was quite a challenge!*

After I got over the initial shock of living there, I was delighted with the profound silence, lapping it up like one who had been dying of thirst. I spent months gazing at the water flowing over the rocks in the creek, becoming increasingly empty until I finally dissolved into nothingness. This felt immensely healing, in fact, it was all I was capable of doing at the time. My daughter went to school thirty miles away and I baked bread, took care of the orchards, canned fruit, and learned to be very still. Whenever we ran out of money, I would simply sell off some of the worldly treasures I had collected from my store years.

Within six months, a story came and would not let me go. It was a fragment of remembrance about a High King in Lemuria. Although I did not really enjoy writing nor did I want to become a writer, I felt that if I wrote a few pages of it down, it would stop bothering me. Well, three chapters later, I realized that it was going to be a book. This became *The Legend of Altazar* which actually took two years to complete. It was an intense process for in order to write, I had to remember. I relived all the experiences in *Altazar* while I was writing it. And it served to complete my lengthy cycle of earthly embodiments. I was finally fully freed from Atlantis, Lemuria, Egypt & AN—all my most cherished earthly memories.

While I was writing *Altazar*, I was also visiting regularly the Og-Min and doing little bits of writing which were merely for my own benefit. I began having dreams and visions of flying with large golden wings, becoming so vast, that I filled the sky over my mountain retreat. This felt wonderfully freeing. Archangel Mikael began to appear, empowering me with a wave of his sword and I began to write messages from him. I started to receive more information from the Angels, some of which has appeared in my little book, *Invoking Your Celestial Guardians*. The Angels kept asking me to acknowledge their Presence and bring them in. I thought I was doing this, although I still perceived them as separate from me.

Then a friend of mine who was a psychic living in Texas, was going through a small financial crisis. So to help her out, I asked her to do a reading for me, although I was not particularly desirous for one at the time. I made up a list of questions and sent them to her with a check. A few weeks later, she called me to say that she had just sent the tape and that it was one of the weirdest readings she had ever given. Apparently she had started the session with her usual guides, when an eight foot tall Golden Angel, who stated that he was the voice of my authority, had taken over the reading!

When the tape arrived, I hurriedly ran to the tape player. Sure enough, she began the reading in her soft voice when all of a sudden, her voice boomed out powerfully in the voice of my Golden Angel. He stated that it was of utmost importance that I not only acknowledge him, but that I bring him in and embody him, that in truth, we were not separate.

Then something clicked inside for me, kind of like the proverbial bolt of lightening. *I realized that we are the Angels!* Looking back on all the writings which I had received over the past year, I saw that the Angels had been trying to tell me this all along. I just hadn't understood. How simple it was!

During this time, I had been put in touch with Jose Argüelles who urged me to attend a spiritual conference in Boulder, Colorado in one month. Although I had never attended either conferences or workshops, I knew that I was supposed to go. Even worse, it soon became clear to me that at this conference I was going to end up speaking on the Angels. Talk about sheer terror! Remember, I was still deeply into my hermit phase.

Knowing that I had only one month to prepare myself, I began to call upon my Golden Angel. Right away, I could feel the most wondrous Golden Light surround me with waves upon waves of Love. Next, I asked my Angel for its name and received the name Solaris Antari. This was the male aspect of my Golden Angel, the one who had appeared to my friend in Texas. At first, I didn't like the name. I was sure that I had read it in some book, so I spent a whole day pouring through my library searching for the name. Of course, it couldn't be found. Repeatedly I asked my Angel for its name and always I received Solaris Antari. *I do have a stubborn streak.*

At last, I accepted my name as Solaris Antari and

began to say, "I am Solaris Antari." Whenever I did this,
I could feel the most loving Golden Presence enter my
physical body. I felt more myself than ever before. I
began writing as Solaris Antari which helped me to
integrate the Celestial energies within my being. A few
weeks later, I received the name Solara Antara,
recognizing this as the feminine aspect of the Angel that
I am.

When I went to Colorado, I was immediately
introduced to some fascinating people with whom I felt a
strong connection, helping me to overcome my shyness.
The conference lasted for three days and I waited until
the last day to approach the man in charge to see if I
could speak. At first, he said that it was impossible;
they were too tightly scheduled as it was. Then as I
repeated to him that I *must* speak and didn't require
much time, he told me to stay in the conference hall and
if anything opened up he would introduce me.

Now the real fear began since I had no idea what I
was going to say. I told my Angel that it had better
know what we were going to speak on, because I didn't.
Talk about surrendering control! The next speaker was
late, the first time this had happened all weekend. The
next thing I knew, I'm being introduced. Walking to the
podium, I thought I was going to have a heart attack
any second, if I didn't simply faint away. There I was,
standing before 350 people including some very well
known New Age teachers, ready to die, or at the very
least, make a total fool of myself. It was not fun.

I began by reading one of my writings from Solaris
Antari. Part of the way through, my Angelic Presence
came in and anchored deeply. A tremendous Love filled
my being as I began to speak about Angels. I noticed
several people crying in the audience. Then my time
was up. I thanked everyone and left the room. Several
people followed me to the hallway with tears streaming
down their faces, asking me to tell them more. This
continued all day. In the afternoon I was given another
opportunity to speak and many people wanted copies of

the Angelic Messages I had written. My Angelic Presence remained firmly anchored inside. It was an amazing experience!

The following day on my flight home, I vowed never to speak publicly about Angels again until I was impeccable within my own being. I felt that the power of this information was similar to throwing the match that starts a prairie fire. And I was told that I had two weeks to put together a book on Angels.

To make an endless story as brief as possible, I'll simply mention that two weeks later when my book, *Invoking Your Celestial Guardians* was at the printers, *(I did get it done on time; I'm very obedient and hardworking.)*, I was forced to move from my house due to a severe allergic reaction to an insect bite. At the time, I had no intention of moving, nowhere that was calling me to come. Also, remember the five cats, one large dog & daughter! It also didn't seem to matter that I owned my house and had little money to move.

So off my daughter and I went in the car with a box of my new Angel books and ended up in Mount Shasta, California three weeks later. Mt. Shasta affected me with all the subtlety of a sledgehammer. I had expected to be greeted by Celestial Choirs upon my arrival at the sacred vortex. Instead, the first sight of the volcano from the highway almost made me sick to my stomach. I could barely drive. Its energy was powerful and unrelenting.

By the time we got settled into our motel we noticed one of those classic lenticular clouds doing some peculiar movements over the pyramid shaped cinder cone of Black Butte; then we really knew we were in for it! That night the Mountain dispassionately informed me that it had claimed me and was going to turn me inside out. Which over the next two years, it did. Most of this process was not fun or filled with ease; it was painful, awkward and difficult, while occasionally laced with moments of exquisite exaltation, so I'd know that I was in the right place. *Not that I didn't often think wistfully of escaping.*

To be fair, I had many magical days upon that mountain. Hiking in shorts, T-shirt, and thin cotton Chinese shoes through snow and ice, onwards on my quest, only to encounter real hikers in woolen pants, hiking boots and crampons, whatever they are! They tended to regard me as suspiciously as a wayward Sasquatch, or perhaps someone who had escaped from the secret chambers within the mountain.

Sometimes I would just sit quietly on a rock, not really thinking or meditating or anything, and the next thing I would remember, with dim recollection, was that I was an individualized unit of consciousness. Then I would have to retrace my path back to this planet in order to discover where I was in the present time and space continuum. *(I still don't know where I went during these experiences, or how they were triggered, but they happened frequently, and always when totally unexpected.)*

Once, while climbing on some rocks, I found a sparkly boulder with large, embossed wing imprints in it. Each feather was carefully delineated, as though seared into the stone. *(Luckily, this time I had a witness with me.)* Later that day, I lay down on slabs of rock and melted into them, becoming vast, when all of a sudden something flew rapidly across my spine which reacted in an electrical burst of Kundalini energy, jolting me back into my body. Opening my eyes, I discovered that a hummingbird had flown over me.

I was told that my experiences on the mountain represented a great earthly initiation, but I have to admit that I was immensely relieved when they were over. I knew that we all have the free will to choose what we wish to experience, and that somewhere deep inside, I had called for this. I was well aware that the lessons of Mount Shasta would be profound; therefore, I resolved to see them through to completion.

After a year, I finally published *The Legend of Altazar* and reprinted my Angel book and now I knew that the hermit had to go out into the world. As I had not spoken publicly since the conference in Colorado and had never given workshops, I wasn't sure how to go about this appointed task. Immediately, I received an invitation from a healer in Houston, Texas who had read my Angel book, to come and give three talks and a full weekend workshop. It was time for panic again! All I could do was call to my Angel and ask it to show me what to do.

Off I flew to Houston which I had never visited before. Here I was shown warm hospitality and support. For my first night's talk, I had prepared a sixteen page speech. What happened is that I read the first paragraph, then set it aside as my Angelic Presence settled deeply inside. After that, I just started talking, not unconsciously or in a trance, but more fully awakened than I normally experience in everyday life. The next two talks went smoothly without any notes.

For the workshop, I had composed a loose schedule as a safety net, with items like: 11:00—balance & center. Of course, I had no idea what this meant. When 11:00 came, I had everyone stand up and then we began the first Star Alignment, which has since refined itself into one of our favorite workshop practices. The entire workshop flowed effortlessly on a beam of Golden Love.

What I mean to convey by all this is that by embodying our Angelic Presence, it's easy to tap into hitherto unexplored parts of our beings. We become limitless and are able to do many things that we have not experienced before, with a new joy and ease. Believe me, if you are an advocate of the lazy way, this is it!

Since then, I have never, ever prepared myself for a talk or workshop other than getting dressed fancier than usual. I simply feel the energy and go with the flow. The Angelic Vortex is always in position when I begin. There is a palpable Golden Light that permeates the room. I don't really consciously do anything to create it. I'm simply there and it's there too. See, how easy! Remember, it's not just my Angel or *the Angel that I am,* who is present, but each of your Angels are present too, and wanting you to feel their Presence. When you get that many Angels together, the energy is magnified and uplifted as we are enfolded into greater Oneness.

I feel exceedingly blessed to know that I am an Angel and can fulfill myself on this planet by helping to awaken other Angels and watch them blossom and transform. My life is not perfect as yet, for I am in human embodiment. I still get sad, discouraged, and impatient like everyone else. At least in this regard, I am normal. Regardless of the current fluctuation of my emotions, I know who I am and why I am here. I know that I am not alone, that there are millions of us on Earth awakening daily, united in the common task of the transcendence of duality. My commitment to fully embody my truest, Highest Self is total. And I joyfully know that I am on the Accelerated Path Homeward.

Therefore, in spite of my heavy workload and my occasional loneliness or weariness, I receive tremendous solace and healing from the Presence of my Golden Solar Angel, the vaster portion of my being, who ever resides within me, loving me unconditionally, encouraging me onwards, returning me Home.

I Am Solara Antara:

I am the eye of the Great Central Sun.
I come from the One.
Within my heart dwells both
Golden winged lion and crystal deer.
To Earth came I on a Golden Beam of Light
Which was the breath of the One.
I am here to See with Clarity,
I am here to manifest the fullness of that which I am
Until there is no more separation between All That Is
And you, its mirrored reflection.
I am simply an open doorway,
Connecting the seen with the Unseen.
A Golden Ray of Love from Above.
In truth, I have no form,
Only a concentration of pulsating Light
Defines my Presence.
Although I may yet appear as separate from you,
I am not.
That I exist as anything definable
Is simply an illusion,
For I reside in the formless ocean of Essence.
Together, we are the One.

Golden Solar Angels

Throughout history, much has been written and experienced about Angels.

Angels are known to Moslems as *Barakas*, to Chinese as *Shiens*, to Hindus as *Devas* and to Native Americans as the *Bird Tribes*. They play an important role in the Bible. There is no doubt as to their existence both on this planet and within the Heavenly Realms. Throughout recorded time, Angels have appeared to humanity as Messengers from God and Instruments of Divine Intervention.

On a more personal level, the Angelic Presence has often been perceived by us as a splendid Guardian Angel. Many of us have had direct experience with our own Guardian Angels beginning when we were young children. Often we have felt loved, guided, protected and inspired through the help of our Guardian Angel.

Radiant, loving Angels have always walked among us upon this planet. During our numerous incarnations our personal Guardian Angel has never left our side. We have never been separate from the One, even when we have felt ourselves to be alone and abandoned. Today there is a greater awareness of the Presence of our Guardian Angels and many are contacting their Angel and receiving its guidance and protection.

**What has not been understood until now is
our own direct relationship with the Angels,
which is far more intimate than we have
previously realized. In truth, Angels are not
separate from us; they are our own Higher
Selves.**

It's important to understand that *your Guardian
Angel is you!* This is not merely your Higher Self, but it
is the vast majority of who and what you truly are!

To fully understand this is the quantum leap of
initiation into mastery and empowerment which leads
to our graduation from duality. If you can acknowledge
your Guardian Angel as a fuller manifestation of the
Truth of your Being, *not separate from you,* then you
shall experience a profound transformation which will
affect all levels of your life.

**The Golden Solar Angels are that part of
ourselves who remained Home, united with
Source.**

They emanate from the Great Central Sun which is
the *Star That We Are.* These Golden Angels created our
little ego selves who have experienced the cycle of embodiments on planet Earth. They did this by sending
earthward a Golden shaft of Light which embedded into
the planet as a tiny starseed. This starseed is merely a
holographic projection of our vast Angelic Self or *Starry
Overself.* It is this starseed which flowered into our
human selves. Yet contained within each of us is a
pre-encoded memory of who we really are. This is also
our map Home. This starseed has always been within
us, even throughout our long ages of forgetfulness.

The Golden Beam of Light connecting our human
self with our Angelic Self has constantly remained in
position as well. It can be perceived as a long Golden
Cord which emanates out of the top of our human heads

and travels all the way to our vast Starry, Angelic Self. Thus have we remained ever connected with our Greater Self.

The more you are willing to bring in and embody your Angelic Presence, the more shall you be transformed.

Your Angel must be anchored all the way down to the toes of your physical body. What this does is greatly facilitate the union of spirit and matter within you. It reactivates your pre-encoded cellular memory banks, granting you fuller access to realms previously veiled. You shall experience the shift into a multi-dimensional state of consciousness giving you greater freedom and ease in your dealings with the the world of duality. As we are fond of saying, *"You shall glide through life on Golden Wings of Light!"*

You will be healed from the conflicts of duality, wherein you were always denying some part of yourself in order to give expression to another facet of your totality. The gap between spiritual and physical planes shall narrow into nothingness. They will be irrevocably joined together in Sacred Union. Head and heart, will and mind, shall be as One.

Your physical body will become rejuvenated and revitalized. You will begin to enjoy expressing yourself in your physical vehicle, if you didn't before. A whole new dance of life will begin as your Light Body and physical body merge together, bringing a lightness of being to everyday life. Your glorious physical body shall truly become a starry temple. Thus you will welcome each day, each breath, as a wondrous new beginning.

Your Years of Tears shall dissolve in the embrace of Love from Above. Within your heart a fountain of Love will open, endlessly recycling waves upon waves of All Encompassing Love. Not only will your ability to love and honor others be greatly enhanced, but you will now be able to receive the abundance of Love directed towards you. Most importantly, you will finally love and honor yourselves. How long have we waited for this step! It is essential that we love ourselves before we direct our love outwards, for are we not all facets of the same glorious One?

Science acknowledges that we currently use only about 10% of our brains; this represents the tiny portion of our consciousness that we utilize during earthly embodiments as our separate, ego driven selves. Once we merge with our Golden Solar Angel, we are given the key to limitlessness and are able to tap into vast realms of previouly unaccessed knowledge and experience. It has been like playing cards with only a tenth of the deck; wouldn't it be easier and more fulfilling to use the whole deck! This can be achieved by merging with the vaster part of ourself, our Golden Angel.

Take a moment if you will, and imagine that tonight while you are asleep something extraordinary happens. It may appear in the form of a dream or vision, but however it manifests, in the morning you shall be irrevocably changed. Because now you know, beyond a shadow of a doubt, that *you are an Angel, consciously serving on this planet to anchor Oneness!*

So what do you do? Probably you won't jump up, quit your job, dump your partner and start wearing long white robes. *(Or maybe you will, possibly that could be appropriate for you.)* Most likely, what you will do is the same thing you do every morning. Get out of bed, go into the bathroom, splash some water on your face, brush your teeth, glance into the mirror and ! ! ! Something is different!

It's not that you look younger, although you might. No, it's the Light streaming out of the face looking back at you. And it's the starry eyes emanating a powerful wisdom and love. You realize that this beautiful being *is* You! That's what you looked like all along, only you had forgotten how exquisitely radiant you truly are.

This is just the beginning of becoming an Angel. Now it's time to go to work or wherever you go out in the world. You can still drive a car, in fact you seem to be driving it effortlessly and even snarled traffic doesn't perturb you the way it used to. You start to notice that people out there, whom you don't even know, are being friendlier than usual, waving and smiling at you. Arriving at your destination, you discover that your day goes by easily as if on a Golden Beam of Light.

Situations that you would previously label as difficult begin to go through almost miraculous transformations, as conflicts resolve themselves effortlessly. All you have to do is keep remembering who you truly are.

There will be times when you forget and become embedded back into the morass and suffering of duality, but that's alright too; it's simply part of the human condition. When this happens, just perceive your situation with clarity and as soon as you can, realign with your Angelic Presence.

Your relationships are also going to transform. From being around your Golden Light, people are either going to be attracted to or repelled by you. This condition simply is. You will find that many people will be awakened and energized by being around you, without your having to do or say anything special. Your Angelic Presence will serve to bring their own Angels closer to them.

These are just a few of the many changes that you might notice the first day that you acknowledge that you are an Angel. Be prepared to discover that Angels are everywhere. As you come out of the closet, it shall give others the courage to be openly that which they truly are.

One of the most profoundly moving experiences of my life took place in June 1988 at an event called Star*Link which was held in the Los Angeles Coliseum. As I was speaking, I asked those in the audience who truly knew, *consciously*, beyond the shadow of a doubt, that they were Angels serving on this sweet Earth, to please stand up. I expected a hundred or so people to respond out of the thousands present. When practically the entire audience stood up with a surge of commitment, my eyes welled up with tears and I could not speak.

Thus it is important for all of us to remember, myself included *and I meet a lot of Angels*, that there are far more of us who know that we are Angels than any of us yet realize! And more are awakening daily. It shall become increasingly important for us to gather together in Angelic Reunions, celebrations, events or whatever, in order to make our Unified Presence felt. For that is what we chose to come here to do.

It is such a profound relief to be able to openly be ourselves here on Earth.

We used to think that we had to go somewhere else or return Home in order to experience our true beingness, but that is simply not true. The deep longing to fully embody our wholeness has propelled us to reawaken and remember. It is that grain of sand in the oyster which births the pearl. And after you and your Angel reunite, you become that shining pearl.

Devas & Healing Angels

There is a difference in focus of emanation between Golden Solar Angels and Devic Angels.

Devas could be said to be the Angelic Presence of plants, minerals, animals, lakes, mountains, cities, countries, planets, etc. Therefore, they represent the Higher Self or collective being of their particular area of focus. The same could be said of Healing Angels, each of whom has chosen a specific area of service, such as the Angel of Compassion or the Angel of Measles.

Although each of these various, wondrous Devas and Angels of Healing also originate as a Golden Ray of *the Star That We Are*, they do not represent our own personal, direct link back to the One. They work with our Golden Solar Angels or Angelic Presence, side by side, rather than in direct vertical alignment. While ultimately, they are not separate from us, as we are ever united in Oneness, Devas are present to serve their chosen purposes alongside us, rather than within us.

Often we are called to work together in service to this planet. We can achieve this much more effectively when we serve together as Angel with Angel, rather than as Angel with third dimensional human, for the scope of our influence is infinitely greater. It is wonderful when we come together, for by calling upon the help of Devas and Healing Angels, we are in effect, calling upon the Angelic Presence of other life forms upon Earth, thereby strengthening the Angelic Connection for all.

It is important that when we ask for their aid, we remember who we are and do not slip back into the illusion of being helpless little humans crying out to something outside of us for help and assistance. Let us serve this planet as awakened, empowered beings, consciously knowing that we are Angels.

Devas and Healing Angels have ever been among us as our Golden Angel has been and it is such a glorious blessing that now we can finally join together to transform this planet. And let us remember that everything on Earth has an Angelic Presence who is patiently waiting to be acknowledged and invoked.

A Message to Humanity from the Golden Angels for 1988

My Beloved Ones,

The door has been opened and you who hear these words have hereby walked through, thus entering upon a new pathway. This path is the Golden Stairway which leadeth Home.

Ask not, "How do I go there?", for in order to return Home—one departs not, but arrives. One does not go out, but comes in. Truly we say unto you, that now is the time to come in.

Enter yourself and merge together your timeless Essence with the fragment of you seemingly encased in the third dimensional world of matter. Unite with the Angel who has long protected, inspired and guided you and know that *this Angel is you.*

This sacred merger, this Divine Union, this interlocking must take place before you can embark upon your journey up the Golden Stairway. In order to rise up, you must first come in completely and reconnect *consciously* with all parts of yourself hitherto denied.

Within this inner union, you shall be empowered. You will be complete as the male / female is wedded within you. You will become an activated, interconnected bridge between spirit and matter.

Thus are the Pillars of Light created. Remember that they are you. Beloved Brethren, you shall be as Rays of Light beaming forth from the Great Central Sun, illuminating, purifying and blessing everything within your sphere.

With the enactment of what was termed the Harmonic Convergence came the birth of the fourth dimension on planet Earth. Now as you enter upon the great year of 1988, please note that this year is when multi-dimensionality shall truly make its Presence felt upon the physical plane.

In this momentous year, duality shall further fade and falter. Yet, within that inevitable crumbling will flower the seeds of the new Divine Dispensation for humanity. You, my dear ones, are these flowers. Nourish your plants and tend them with loving tenderness, for each of you is needed for the fulfillment of the Divine Plan on Earth.

During this time there shall be a massive awakening and quickening of consciousness. Many of the pre-encoded memories implanted deep within your cellular patterning in a time capsule form long ago will be reactivated.

There will be a great stirring and soaring as you begin to remember. You shall remember far beyond the sphere of earthly embodiments. You will reach out to the stars, the most distant stars, to dimensional universes yet unknown to conscious memory. For within the secrets of the stars lies humanity's true origins and purpose.

All of this shall await you on your journey up the Golden Stairway. So fear not as you walk softly in this year of Manifest Destiny. For you will not walk alone. The Starry Families do indeed gather together and reunite. The pathway which you tread together is composed of purest Golden Light.

The arduous process of restructurization has passed its critical point for many of you. Now your steps will become surer and Lighter. You have made your decision and your choice has been to begin the Accelerated Path Homeward. This is achieved by coming into balance on all levels.

Awakened humanity of planet Earth, you have done your work well. We ever stand beside you, above you and within you. We offer you our encouragement, support, All Encompassing Love and above all, the certainty of achieving your goal. This is your year. Prepare to emerge, prepare to succeed and flourish, and prepare to fly!

Angelic Names

By now you may be interested in contacting and embodying your Golden Solar Angel, but you might assume that the process is lengthy and difficult. Instead, it is amazingly simple!

Remember that the Golden Angels want to be merged with us, hence they call and encourage us to bring them in. All you have to do is sincerely call out to your Angel, letting it know that you acknowledge and welcome its Presence, that you are now ready to anchor and embody your full Higher Self.

You may ask your Angel for its name, *your* name. These names are not in English or any other recognizable Earth language, for Angels come from the stars. This name could be termed your multi-dimensional or starry name. And once received and used, the resonance of its vibration will serve to trigger and reactivate your pre-encoded cellular memories, allowing you to receive and harmonize with ever higher frequency energy fields.

Due to the fact that the Golden, Solar Angels emanate from a sphere beyond duality, they are androgynous in nature.

What this means is that their male / female polarities have already united. Since we often have difficulty in relating personally with an *it* or *they*, our Angels usually appear to us in either a male or female form. When you receive your Angelic Name, you may receive either the male or female polarity. Often this is soon followed by the name of the other polarity. Sometimes, you will hear the name of its Unified Presence, receiving one name representing both aspects of your Angel. Simply accept the perfection of what you receive.

On occasion, one will not receive their Angelic Name. Instead you will hear what I term a *trigger name.* Remember, that some of these Angels originate from very far away. Sometimes it takes awhile to shift your consciousness to the necessary octave in order to receive these heightened vibratory frequencies. If you receive a name that doesn't feel quite right, perhaps part of it is in English or Italian or whatever, accept it as your *trigger name* and work with it. It will help you to step up your energies to the dimensional octave where you will find your name. Receiving your Angelic Name from your trigger name can happen in a matter of minutes or months. Once again, it doesn't matter. Everything is unfolding perfectly. Your Angelic Presence is in charge of this process, not you or me.

There is great importance in receiving your Angelic Name yourself.

Many people ask me to give them a name and although this would perhaps be easier, it would not be correct. That is the old way of doing things, when we received our spiritual knowledge horizontally or second hand. Now we are returning to the place of the beginning and once more, we are learning to receive directly from the One. This is the purest and cleanest way possible and is open to all of us. The reunion is between you and your Higher Self. Beings like me merely serve as facilitators in the process. We can hold open the doorways, but you are the ones who must enter. The process of contacting your Angel and receiving your name confers great empowerment upon you. This empowerment with its subsequent evolution into mastery is one of the great gifts which the Golden Solar Angels bring.

I cannot stress strongly enough how important it is that you *trust* what you hear. From countless experiences during the initiation process in our workshops on Angelic Awakening, I have encountered many people who feel that they didn't receive their name (*with the resulting sense of disappointment and failure*) who when taken further, realize that they had their name all along. Sometimes it pops into your head so easily that you think that it simply can't be the one. Or like me, you think that you must have heard it somewhere else and you don't want to copy someone else's name. But often it turns out that the reason it was so familiar is because it is *your* name!

If you have received more than one word for your name, this denotes your various star lineages. These could be perceived as the Golden Rays which lead back to the One. You might discover others who share part of your name. These people share a Golden Ray with you. They have traveled with you for quite a distance, united as small fragments of star.

One thing that I constantly find fascinating is the linked resonance of Angel Names, most of which are highly unusual. It's wonderful how Angels in North Carolina and Angels in Finland receive such similar names when they have never heard anything like them before!

Once we receive our name, we can begin to translate it, for each name has a significant meaning which is a major key to our chosen Mission on the planet. To discover the translation of your name, all you need to do is to ask your Angel. You can also find the symbol for your name which may be a powerful trigger. Some have even received their starry signature which has opened the doors to star writing which some are beginning to receive and translate. In other words, there's a whole universe of discovery inherent in your Angelic Name.

The Angelic Name is the bridge between us as humans and us as stars.

We also have an even truer Starry Name which is difficult to speak with the third dimensional physical vehicle. Some awakened Angels have received names which are extremely close to their Starry Names; usually they are the only ones who can pronounce them correctly. These Starry Names are exceedingly beautiful in an other-worldly sense.

The more that you let your Angelic Name resonate throughout your being, increasingly will you experience a profound transformation within your entire being. You will be quickened by a very beautiful cellular restructurization. This will enable you to receive the magnificent Golden Angelic frequencies, many of which have never before been available on this planet. As your Angelic Name is spoken, it sends forth sound currents which recalibrate the harmonic resonance of the whole planet. Most importantly, your Angelic Name is the Golden Ray which links you to the One. Embodying your Angel is your passport to travel within this Ray on the Accelerated Path Homeward.

Claiming Your Name

I urge all of you to seek your name.

You can begin by visualizing a brilliant Golden White Star above you. This is *the Star that We Are.* It could also be called God or the One. Breathe in the Golden Light from the Star. See yourself as a pillar of Golden White Light. Be sure to bring the energy down all the way to your toes. Fill your entire being with Golden White Light until you become that Light.

Now ask your Angel, *the Angel that you truly are,* to sound your name to you. Open yourself up and surrender all preconceptions, allowing yourself to receive the name. You may receive one or several words. They will be different from anything you have heard before and strikingly familiar at the same time. You may receive either the male or female aspect of your Angel or both in a combined form. You will receive what is perfect for you at this exact moment in time.

When you hear your name, you might want to try it on and claim it. The first time you begin from the Golden White Star above you and bring the vibration all the way down to the toes of your physical body, stating out loud, "I am *(your name.)*" Let the sound resonate deeply within you.

It might feel a little awkward at first. Some people

experience a rush of energy or tingling in their body. This is because you are bringing in a new frequency of energy into your physical form. It's like buying a new pair of cowboy boots, they are stiff at first, but the more you wear them, the more comfortable they become.

As you increasingly try on these higher dimensional frequencies within your being, the more your internal cellular structure shall be realigned. Your Angelic Name is your individual trigger, your personal resonance to anchor multi-dimensionality within you.

As you state your name again, this time claim it across the universe, bringing it once more into the toes of your body. This anchors yet more of your vastness while further merging Heaven into Earth.

The third time, you are going to call out your name from the heart of the Great Central Sun and anchor it deeply into the toes of your formerly 3D body. Now you are beginning to get a real taste of the vastness of your Angelic Self. This brings the Light Body into the physical body, merging them together into conscious multi-dimensionality.

And remember, the more you use your name, the more powerful it becomes. The vibrations of your Angelic Name anchor within you those exquisite Angelic Frequencies. Many of us have chosen to use our Angelic Names all the time, helping us to claim and ground the fullness of our Presence as we move through everyday life. Often when I find myself in difficult situations, like driving my car on a treacherous icy road, I will begin to sing my name over and over. My fear quickly dissolves as my Angelic Presence strengthens while and em-powerment and clarity returns.

Twelve Steps to Unite with your Golden Angel

1. Create Your Space

Find a peaceful place where you feel comfortable and protected. You can make it even more beautiful by adding crystals, flowers & lighting a candle. You can prepare yourself by bathing and putting on clean clothes. You might want to play some inspiring music to help get you in the mood.

2. Quiet Your Mind

After you enter your sacred space where you feel safe and protected, empty your mind by gently letting go of your doubts and fears, then center your being through breathing, stretching, or meditating. Let your thoughts and anxieties slowly drift away.

3. Visualize The Star

Above you is a radiant Golden White Star which showers you with Golden Light. Feel this Light enter your body through the crown of your head. Let yourself be filled with Golden Light from your Star. Breathe in the Golden Light to all the fibers and cells of your being. Now, feel yourself radiating as a Golden Beam of the Star. You and your Star have become One.

4. Attune With Your Angel

Remember, your Angel is always with you. It has never left your side. To feel your Angelic Presence, all you need do is remember that it is present. Now you will start feeling the Angelic frequencies which ever surround you. Feel yourself embraced by Golden Wings of All Encompassing Love.

5. Send Forth The Call

Call out to your Angel, sending it deep gratitude for always being with you, for guiding & protecting you and for loving you even when you were unable to love yourself. Speak to your Angel of your yearning to fully feel its Presence and to reunite, that you may be whole once again.

6. Listen And Feel

Feel the waves of Golden Light which surround you in ever increasing brilliance. Then allow yourself to experience the Love and delight which your Angel directs towards you. Simply bask in it; swim in this Golden River of Love and drink deeply.

7. Ask For Your Name

This is the time to ask your Angel for its name, *your* name, that you may bring it in and become One.

8. Listen And Trust

Simply open yourself to receive the sounds which your Angel is sending to you. Do not allow your mind to interfere, gently set it aside whenever it tries to intrude. If necessary, ask your Angel to make your name louder or clearer. It shall do this, for it wants you to receive your name. As your name comes to you, trust what you are hearing.

9. Try On Your Name

Speak your Angelic Name and let it resonate throughout you. Notice how it feels inside of your being as you bring in the higher dimensional frequencies. The more you say it, the more comfortable it will be, and the more empowered you shall feel.

10. Claim Your Name

Say out loud, "I am (*your name*)." As you do this you will bring the energy down from the Golden, White Star above you all the way to your toes. As you repeat this process several times, the Golden Beam of Light will be anchored deeply into your physical body. This is Angelic Grounding.

11. Merge With Your Angel

Feel your Angel descend into your body and merge with you chakra by chakra until heart is aligned with heart, mind with mind, will with will, toes with toes, eyes with eyes, until you have truly become One.

12. Go Forth Freely

Now you are ready to embody your Angelic Presence. Remember that you are an Angel, consciously serving on this Earth, no matter where you are or what you are doing. This will transform your entire life in wondrous ways!

I Am Metatron:

Beloved Angels of Earth, we approach you now in order to announce our closeness to you. The veils of separation have been rent. The only thing that keeps us apart are your outmoded thought forms which hold onto the illusion of duality.

We are nearer than you imagine. In fact, you may find us inside of you, as part of you, as you are also found inside of us. Have we not told you that separation is an illusion! Nothing is outside of you; nothing is separate from the One. Bring this truth deep inside your being and embed it there until you know this without a shred of doubt.

The doorways are now wide open. This is why the ancient mysteries are no longer shrouded in the mists of time for those who dare to ask the proper questions. This is why the Highest Beings of Light do speak out clearly to those who remember to call.

Everything is open to you, dear Angels on Earth. We shall do all that we can to facilitate the fulfillment and completion of your Divine Mission.

The marriage of spirit and matter takes place within your physical bodies. The Earth is healed and liberated through this process of Sacred Union. Therefore, it is of utmost importance that you fulfill your sacred tasks as multi-dimensional bridges, as living embodiments of spirit-pcharged matter. Indeed, that is why you chose to come to Earth.

As your Light Body merges with your physical body, your Love expands and you become more yourself than before. As you grow and transform, duality's hold upon you diminishes. This means that you become less of a tightly bundled, limited, individualized unit of consciousness. As you rise more fully into the truth of your being, you will enter the level of awareness that simply stated is: *I am the One; I am the Many.*

The Angel on the Television

On Friday, August 14th, 1987, a few days before Harmonic Convergence, a couple in Mount Shasta, California turned on their television to watch the evening news. I had never met them, but they had just read my small book, *Invoking Your Celestial Guardians* and had talked about contacting their Angels for several days.

When they turned on their television set, there was a sudden, brilliant flash of light, then the figure of an Angel appeared. This Angel was in the form of a Light Being with beautiful outstretched wings. Her heart chakra was a lavender pink and radiated outwards in concentric rainbow colored patterns of Light. When you put your hand near the Angel, double helix spirals would emerge from her. The Angel's energy could be felt as tingling pulsations of energy currents which traveled up your arms and dispersed throughout your body.

The astonishing appearance of this Angel caused quite a stir, especially since thousands were gathering in Mt. Shasta for Harmonic Convergence. Soon there were lines of people extending around the block waiting for hours to view the Angel. Tour buses began arriving in the quiet residential street where this had occurred.

National media showed up in droves. The story was covered by the major television networks and many magazines and newspapers.

The woman who owned the television set initially appeared to be an unlikely sort for this to happen to. She is strong *(some would say tough)* the mother of teenagers, who is fond of loud rock and roll and lots of make up, not your typical airy fairy spiritual type. But she was perfectly chosen to be responsible for protecting the Angel, for she is unshakably honest, grounded, and not susceptible to ego's inflation.

When I returned from my Convergence trip to a remote lake, I received an invitation to visit the Angel and channel it. At first I was somewhat skeptical, as I often am about phenomena until I can feel it out myself. Entering the room, I could feel the Angel's immense loving Presence which filled me with gratitude. I could sense the deep concentration necessary in order for her to manifest into third dimensional density. This moved me deeply. There was tremendous love present in that room.

Late at night after everyone had left, I sat quietly meditating in front of the television set, making myself empty. Then silently communing with the Angel, I asked her what she wanted to communicate. This is what I wrote:

A Message from the Angel on the Television

BELOVED humanity of planet Earth, I am the Angel of the Presence. I am the Angel who is found within the heart of Essence of each of you. I am the Angel who containeth all Angels, as a bouquet containeth myriad blossoms united together into one glorious display. I am the One; I am the Many. I am the Angel of the Presence.

I have appeared before you now because you are finally ready to receive me. I have come as the Herald of the resplendent Golden Dawn which doth arise. I have come to announce the birth of Heaven upon Earth. *Above all, I have come to issue the Call for the Angels within you to awaken.*

As you see me, as you feel my electrical currents pulsate throughout your cells, please allow yourself to bring me inside. I am that which you truly are—a pulsating, shimmering rainbow Being of Light, radiating limitless Love and Harmony. As you perceive these qualities in my image, please recognize them in yourself, *for I am you!*

You might find it amusing that I have appeared to you on a television set, but is this not an appropriate method for us to demonstrate the melding of Heaven and Earth? If Angels can appear in densest matter, then we have clearly manifested the penetration of Spirit into the third dimensional world. This breakthrough represents a quantum leap in consciousness by humanity, for a major doorway has thus been opened. This has been made possible by your devoted, collective efforts in transmuting the previous levels of density. We of the Angelic Realms shower you with loving gratitude for helping us to penetrate the doorway between Spirit and Matter and birth the New Age!

The place of this penetration is within the Heart. See the expanding rays of Light emanating from my heart center. Bring me within you and feel your vast heart expand and radiate with mine. My beloved ones, know you of the vast Love I and my Angelic Brethren have for all humanity? It is limitless and unconditional. It is Love merged with Wisdom, innocent and pure. Let our Love penetrate your beings and revitalize your cellular structures. Let our Love fling open your hearts. Let our Light free you from the bondage of the illusion of separation. For as I am the One and the Many—so are you.

I, the Angel of the Presence, shall be appearing in many third dimensional guises. Look for me on your computer screens, your television sets and beaming down from your satellites. Look upwards and you shall find me in the sky in the form of a cloud. You shall see me in the faces of those you pass by on the street. And if we have fulfilled our mission of service to Earth, you shall recognize me in your mirror, in the sweetest Love pouring forth from your eyes.

Yes, Dear Ones, Let it be known that the Angels are truly here on Earth ! ! !

About ten days after the Angel first appeared, the house was closed to the public. There was concern that people were beginning to worship the television image instead of looking within and seeing that they were Angels, as the Angel had stated in her message. The television was quietly taken to another dwelling where it could be viewed by those with a real calling to see it. About two years after it first appeared, the television ceased to work. However, if you wish to see the Angel, simply look in your mirror!

Wings & the Light Body

We used to think that the Light Body was something that existed outside and separate from us.

Something that had to be developed through long years of arduous preparations. In fact, we have been wearing our Light Bodies all along, only we just didn't recognize them under all the heavy cloaks and disguises that we have placed over them for aeons. Now all we need do to rediscover our Light Bodies, is to remove the layers of debris with which we covered them up, for it is time to set them free. Let's wear them proudly and without hindrance!

And of course, wings are an emanation of the Light Body and the perfect balance to the energy pouring forth from our chakras. Some people still roll their eyes when we speak openly about wings, but they are there. If you prefer, you can perceive them as energy fields that emanate out of your central back between the shoulder blades, what we call the *wing area*, and extend outwards. They are not dripping with feathers, although they can sometimes be seen that way. Rather, they are aglow with rainbow, iridescent glints of radiating energy pulsations.

During the initiation process in our Angelic Awakening workshops, we have healers who act as wing openers. By seeing the wings, they help activate and expand wings which have sometimes been impacted inside, sort of like an ingrown toenail, and often, just as painful. Most frequently, our wings simply need to be fluffed up after a difficult passage through life. But we have had some fascinating experiences with wings.

Once one of our wing persons observed a man who had upside down wings. Throughout the initiation she tried to correct them, but could not. Interestingly enough, the person with upside down wings had a long history of mental illness.

Some people have two sets of wings with an outer black pair covering the inner Golden ones—maybe they haven't fully committed themselves to the Light. Those of fairy lineage may have huge, gossamer wings like a fairy, quite lacy and delicate. There are those with butterfly wings who have a high frequency fluttery energy.

And of course, sometimes we encounter fallen Angels who have black, pleated, pointy wings. I feel that there is much more to wings than has yet been revealed. I envisage a whole new facet of healing being developed which deals entirely with wings. Already there are some extremely gifted wing healers around.

Wings are an excellent barometer of how your current state of consciousness is riding the waves of the Golden Beam or is being tossed about on the Winds of Change.

So check them out and send them some respectful gratitude for balancing your being and keeping you from falling flat on your face!

Remember, maybe it didn't used to be safe to walk around this planet openly being ourselves. Perhaps, that's why we started throwing those heavy cloaks of judgement and denial over our Light Body. But times have changed, the planet has a new etheric blueprint. We are living under a new Divine Dispensation. Now, whether you're security conscious or not, being openly yourself is the safest way to be!

The Golden Eagle Flies

The Golden Eagle flies
Heavenward . . .
And as he soars
Ever towards the sun,
He looks not backwards,
His gaze moves not
Side to side,
Focusing forward
To the welcoming Light.

Passing through clouds of storm,
They deter him not,
Neither rain nor wind

Slow his steady flight
Through darkness of night
Until once again,
The new dawn arises
With shining splendor.

The Golden Eagle flies
Homeward . . .
As wings of feather
Transmute into
Wings of Light.
He calls out
And is answered
By Angelic Song.

Those Beings of Light
Surround him now,
Cradling him in purest Love,
Sending forth encouragement,
That he can fly so far,
That he is not alone.

Thus the Golden Eagle flies
Farther than ever before
On Golden Wings of Light
With a new surge of energy
For he has claimed his birthright,

He has activated his empowerment.
Obstacles cease to exist.

There is no limitation here
High above the clouds.
There is only blissful joy
And all-pervading Love
In the radiant beams of Golden Light
Emanating from the One Star.
That is the Source of All.

You too, can be that Golden Eagle
Flying freely through the sky.
Simply surrender to the Call,
You can rise above it all,
And as your feathers fall
They shall serve as beacons
For others to follow.

Transformation

A profound transformation shall affect all levels of your being after you have merged with your Angelic Presence.

This cannot be overstated. Time and again, during numerous workshops and talks, I have seen peoples' lives literally change before my eyes. First there is a deep reawakening as if from a long slumber which, indeed, it has been. Often there are tears of recognition and remembrance. The memories unfold of who you really are and why you chose to come to this planet. Then you remember how you came here and from where. A profound releasing of pain and sorrow is experienced as you realize how perfect the entire process of reawakening has been.

You are now able to look at all facets of your life with heightened clarity of perception. Problems and obstacles which appeared to be unsolvable are eased with the wisdom of fuller understanding. You gain a greater freedom to move smoothly through the mundane aspects of everyday life. The hold of duality loosens greatly. *Truly, you begin to glide through life on Golden Wings of Light!* You gain an increased sense of your Divine Purpose in being incarnate upon Earth during the present age. This enables you to experience a greater sense of fulfillment in everything you do.

On the physical level you will feel tremendous

change. Becoming evermore beautiful as you radiate love and wholeness, you will emanate an aura of timelessness.

You will develop a starry magnetism which shall draw others to you without any conscious effort on your part. Your entire auric field will clear up as you embody vaster amounts of Golden Light.

A new Golden, Solar Spine is in the process of being developed. This is necessary for the full activation of the Light Body. The Golden Spine has twelve chakras, the usual seven plus five more subtle and refined in Essence.

Most wondrous of all, is the fountain of enhanced Love which shall flow through you. This Love serves as a Golden Elixir of healing and rejuvenation.

We used to think of ourselves as containing a little flame of spirit within the heart of our physical bodies. With our enlarged perceptions, we can now see that we are really vast Beings of Light containing small physical bodies. Our entire process of restructurization has served as an alchemical process in which we have repeatedly distilled and refined all of our earthly experiences until they have transformed into one, pure drop of Golden Elixir. This is our true Essence, the Essence of the One. It is this pure drop of Elixir which is the seed for the activation of our One Heart.

A Message to Humanity
from the Golden Angels for 1989

Welcome to the year of Emergence, Activation, & Empowerment! We speak to the awakening humanity of planet Earth who have made their quantum leaps in 1988 and who are now ready to move onward.

This is the year to go forth freely, unhindered by the self imposed limitations of duality. First there shall be a commitment made. This commitment shall be to honor your Highest Truth without compromise, to be an embodiment of your Higher Self, to walk forth openly as the Angel You Truly Are. And to anchor an unshakeable integrity deep within your being. We ask you to make an irrevocable commitment to serving your Higher Purpose. For now is truly the time to step forward and fulfill your Divine Mission on Earth. This mission is to fully embody who you truly are!

We are the Golden Solar Angels who come from Beyond the Beyond. We come as emissaries from the stars, for in truth, we are stars. We come to remind you that you are not separate from us, and that you too, are stars.

We ask you to stand in the radiant Golden Beam of your star and to know within every fiber and cell of your being that you *are* that radiant beam of Golden Light. Thus shall you be empowered!

The gateways are open, the hindrances are past; your old doubts and fears have melted away in the love of self-acceptance. Now you are free to receive fullest support as you step forward on your Golden Beam. FOR YOU ARE THE GOLDEN BEAM!

Together, we are united in one common goal, that of awakening and liberating this planet. Together, we are united as shared Essence of the one great Golden, White Star. By realizing this, we reunite the fragments of our star. And the glue we use is All Encompassing Love!

This is the year when many of your most precious dreams shall manifest and flower. This is the year when you can have it all. This is the year of fulfilled desires. This is the year of gathering together with your greater Starry Families. This is the year when you shall step free of your past, releasing attachments to former embodiments and old thought forms that you may simply embody purest Essence. And this is the year when our Unified Presence shall truly make itself felt.

Beloved humanity of planet Earth, we ever embrace you in penetrating Golden Beams of Heavenly Love. We merge with you in order to affect the transformation of duality, anchoring Heaven deeply into Earth.

We invite you to walk with us as One, for that we truly are. And together we shall continue this grand adventure of the journey Homeward.

The Human Condition

You might assume that once your Angel has been contacted and embodied, that you will now have a life free of struggle or imperfection.

If we were to be perfected beings all the time, we would not be on Earth, rather we would find ourselves back in the Celestial Realms. It is important that we acknowledge and bless our humanness. And inherent in the state of being human and physically incarnate, is what we currently regard as imperfection.

Since we can't become *perfect* overnight, you might wonder why we want to embody our Angelic Presence. First of all, we shall experience a tremendous shift in attitude. While our outer conditions may not transform instantly (*and some might*), our way of meeting these experiences will begin to be drastically altered for the better. Knowing that duality is no longer our predominant reality will give you a greater freedom to move through it lightly. You won't be as entangled in the shimmering veils of illusion.

The doorways to the Beyond shall open, giving you a wider perspective on all aspects of your life. Sometimes you will feel empowered and move through life on a Golden Beam of authority, filled with limitless Love for all of humanity. Other times, you might feel weary and helpless, lost and alone—a temporary return to the old human condition of struggle and suffering.

It is of utmost importance during these times of confusion when you are mired in the morass of despair of ever gaining your freedom that you suspend all judgements upon yourself.

It will help if you can acknowledge that none of us living here upon the Earth is ever given more than a fragment of the Truth. That fragment is the sum total of our great stores of knowledge. If I judged your actions upon my narrow fragment of perception, I would be as much in error as you would be if you judged me by the fragment that you possess. About the only thing that we can safely assume is that every lifeform upon this planet is doing the best that they can at any given time, with their present level of consciousness. Of course, we could all do better simply by liberating ourselves from the illusions of duality and radiating vast Love.

Yet, we are doing the best that we can right now. Maybe in the next instant of time we shall be wiser, but let's accept one another, *without judgement,* and let us learn our own way. Remember, flowers in a field do not bloom at the same time. They are not all the same color and size. Wouldn't it be boring if they were, if there was some decree that said all flowers must be exactly the same shade of pink and bloom for the same two weeks in May. Then the rest of the year would be quite barren. Each of us brings a unique, much needed piece that completes our puzzle of Oneness.

There are times when we are called to serve others as triggers and catalysts of profound change and breakthrough. This is part of what we chose to do here for each other. But even then we must wait for the correct opening to present itself, whether we create it or not. Then we can share of our wisdom freely without anticipation of results or reward, sending our help flying forth freely on the wind to land where they may.

After that, it is the other person's choice what to do with that which we have so lovingly given. Sometimes, it is a long wait before you see any change, for some seeds have a long period of germination. Others lie fallow forever. Whatever happens, your task is complete, you have freely shared yourself; now let go of any expectations.

It's easy to label all aspects of the human condition as inferior to a more spiritual state of peace and inspiration. Yet what we are called upon to do is to embrace our humanness—loving both ourselves and others without judgement when we are exhibiting our human characteristics. This is of utmost importance in order to reach our desired state of Oneness!

We did not choose to come here merely in order to suffer limitation. There are strong benefits to being in human incarnation that we often forget about in our states of judgement and denial.

Human bodies give us opportunities to fully explore our individuality as it leads us on its spiral journey back to Oneness. We get to play with bodies, minds and emotions in the most wondrous ways. And learn from the deep teachings of Nature which is a vast reservoir of knowledge. Life on this planet is a constant adventure of rediscovery.

Matter is not simply heavy density, but it is a magnificent medium for expressing our creativity. Here we are free to play as Gods, manifesting our thoughts and desires endlessly like child's play. If we are not happy with our creations thus far, then we need to raise our aspirations higher, lifting our thoughts and emotions to new octaves of awareness which will then manifest. Isn't that why we came here?

And if we can incorporate the miracle of humor, viewing the human condition with a large dose of laughter instead of taking everything so seriously, won't that lighten everything? This planet is a playground for Gods and Angels in human form. Some of us are playing the roles of "*good guys*" and some of us are the "*bad guys*", but sooner or later, this play of duality is going to be over. After the makeup and costumes are removed, who is going to remain? Just some Celestial Light Beings who finally completed a grand adventure, a tiny cosmic play.

In the meantime, during those days that find you grouchy and mean, or sobbing with tragedy, try to remember what is really happening.

We are being called upon to let go of and complete our entire cycle of earthly embodiments in just a few short years!

Honor the progress we have made. Bless these emotions and experiences. Soon enough you will be graduating from the human condition. And who knows, maybe then we'll discover how much fun it was and be sorry that it's over.

Of course, there will always be a world out there just waiting to be created. The sound of the Celestial Trumpets will resound again throughout the Heavens asking for volunteers in co-creation. Some of us might have forgotten by then how hard it was for us here and remembering only the joy, willingly descend into matter again and again!

Beached Whale Syndrome

**There is yet another state of conscious-
ness which we need to understand and
integrate.**

This is what we Angels call the Beached Whale
Syndrome. It's just like it sounds. When you experience
beached whale you appear to be stranded in duality,
feeling much like a huge whale gasping its last breath
upon an inhospitable rocky shore. Not only is your Angel
nowhere in sight, but your wings have shriveled and
disappeared. You cannot meditate or feel slightly
spiritual. Oh, I forgot to mention the part about the
fountain of love in your heart which has totally dried up.
You get the picture, I'm sure. You've probably experienced this more than a few times.

Whenever this condition occurs it is important to
recognize that you are in *beached whale* and not take
things too personally. Our initial reaction is usually one
of alarm and panic followed by judgement of ourselves for
not being *spiritual*. Please suspend your judgement and
see that *beached whale syndrome* is a necessary part of
the assimilation and integration process.

As we need time to sleep at night in order to integrate our daily activities and explore other planes of consciousness, so we need a break from the input of accelerated spiritual frequencies.

So please enjoy your *beached whale*. Use this time to catch up on your paperwork and movies. It's a good opportunity to focus on the often neglected *mundane* details of life and to simply have fun. You will find that by not struggling with it and instead adopting an attitude of cheerful acceptance that *beached whale syndrome* will pass by quickly and happily. One morning you'll wake up and discover that love has returned!

It is important to remember that there is no facet of our lives or of our beings which is not spiritual or which is separate from the One. By loving all parts of ourselves and all stages of our process, we become whole *and holy*.

There is a cousin of *beached whale* which I call *battered whale* which is even worse. This is when we have taken on the cares of the entire planet. We feel this collective pain and suffering inside our beings. This too, is a natural part of the process of becoming whole. As we increasingly open up to our inherent Oneness, we sometimes internalize the cares and trials of the entire planet to aid in their transmutation.

Many of us have experienced days of crying for no apparent reason. It is my belief that we are shedding our tears for the entire planet and that we take turns doing this for all humanity. At any given moment in time there are always some of us crying for the One. This is a sacred task that we should accept and allow with a greater degree of understanding.

Again, when this occurs it is crucial to remember that what we are experiencing is collective rather than personal. Whether it be tears or anger, simply let these emotions pass freely through you without judgement. By letting them transmute through you, you serve us all.

I used to be extremely bothered by spiritual teachings which indicated that if I was truly living my life correctly and being sufficiently spiritual, that I wouldn't experience any disturbances in my life. Thus I always judged myself as a terrible failure on the path. Now I know that it is alright to be sometimes sad, angry or disheartened, although I prefer not feeling that way. It is part of the human condition. Sooner or later, these emotions shall drop away in the Light of deeper awareness.

It's important to keep everything in a vaster perspective. Just look at how quickly we are reawakening! And how rapidly and thoroughly we are restructuring. Our process of transformation is proceeding quite fast in these accelerated times. Looking back five years or so, many of us can see that we have undergone tremendous changes. We have released many of our old patterns and habits. We have opened our hearts to embrace a universal vision of Oneness.

We are no longer focusing merely on this planet nor this solar system; we have extended our understanding ever beyond. This is the process of retracing our footprints back home.

As we extend our vision to ever larger vistas, our awareness grows increasingly vaster. The star of our being becomes ever larger until it encompasses everything. Then and only then, will we have completed our Divine Missions and returned Home.

Unifying the Polarities

As the male and female aspects of your Golden Angel unite within you, an enhanced state of Oneness permeates your entire being.

You no longer feel lonely, alone or lacking. You are complete within yourself as your own polarities merge within you. Actually, this can be rather romantic at times. You may experience periods of intense bliss when your kundalini is fully activated as the male and female polarities of your Angel unite within you. During these periods of heightened awareness, you feel embraced in the All Encompassing Love of both wings of your Golden Angel. This is pure joy manifest and quite difficult to duplicate thus far in a normal, third dimensional human relationship.

Here is a useful practice to get in touch with your male / female polarities in order to discover how they are doing. First, sit quietly with an object like a crystal or a rock. Place this in your right hand and put your left hand behind you. Now you are able to separate the polarities and bring forth your masculine pole. *(If you are left handed, this process should be reversed.)* Feel the presence of your male polarity. You should be able to quickly see if he is too strong or too weak. Perhaps, there is some fear around your masculine side. You may perceive him as an angry warrior, for example. Or he may need a good dose of empowerment.

Do any healing you feel is necessary to bring him into wholeness. Talk to him, encourage him, love him, make peace with him—whatever it takes. When you feel that your masculine polarity is balanced, then place your crystal in your left hand, putting your right hand behind your back.

Now feel your feminine side. How is she doing? Is she sad, forlorn, angry, manipulative or feeling unappreciated? Give yourself whatever time you need to really get in touch with this part of yourself. Then give her the healing she needs, whether it be soothing nourishment or courage. When your feminine feels in balance, let go of your crystal and place both of your hands in a comfortable position in front of you.

Let your polarities gently come together in harmony and love. It is very important that their energy is equally balanced and complementary. Some examples of unbalanced polarities which I have experienced in workshops are: a beautiful Goddess with a dirty, smelly Viking warrior, a stern Patriarch with a little girl and a male artist with a puppy! Remember, each polarity must be equal with the other. Can you imagine your two polarities living together in a fulfilled love relationship?

If you do this regularly, you will be able to heal any

imbalances before they manifest on the physical plane. And you will be well along on your journey towards wholeness.

Another way to work on this is to visualize the male and female aspects of your Angel, *the Angel You Truly Are,* embracing you with their wings.

Since Golden Solar Angels exist at a higher dimensional octave than we presently do, their polarities are reversed.

You will notice that the female aspect of your Angel resides on your right side while the male aspect is found on your left. *(Again, if you are left-handed this will be reversed.)*

At first, it might be easier to perceive them as outside of you. You can see them embracing and uniting into One Being. After you have done this successfully a few times, you can bring them inside and let them unite within you. This can often trigger a profound experience of pure bliss and sublime ecstasy. *(At the very least, it is deeply romantic!)*

The truth of the matter is that your Angels are in that state of cosmic union inside you all the time. All we need do is open ourselves to experience what already is taking place. Once we do, how can we ever be lonely again?

As your inner polarities come into deeper states of balance, you will notice a profound effect upon your outer life. This is experienced most obviously in the area of relationships.

As you radiate an aura of wholeness, you shall begin to attract to you others who also radiate wholeness. Just as when you came from a place of lack and loneliness, you drew towards you experiences of lack and denial.

In duality opposites attract while in Oneness, like attracts like.

Until you unify the dualities within your whole being, opposites shall continue to attract. Opposites are brought into your life so that you may balance your own polarities. They mirror parts of you that haven't been developed either through denial or lack of interest. Haven't you noticed some couples where one of the partners is immersed in duality while the other is ever striving for Oneness? This is not simply a case of two people caught in duality where one is good, the other bad. Actually, together they are serving to fulfill an alchemical process of balance and transmutation.

Thus far, most relationships that we've experienced on this planet have been karmic. This has entailed a great deal of processing between the individuals involved and often much pain as well. While not particularily enjoyable, they have served to bring us into greater Oneness.

Now it is time for new forms of relationship to manifest. The connection between two people will no longer be karmic in nature. Instead we shall come together in the One Heart, aligning the shared Essence connecting us in love, trust, respect and openness.

We will no longer have to devote a great deal of time and stress to processing imbalances within our relationships. Each of us will be firmly empowered, so there will be no question of giving our power away to another.

Here's my campfire analogy: Living our life and following our spiritual path is like sitting before our own campfire. We constantly tend our fire, adding more wood and stirring the ashes when necessary. Thus we keep our campfire going. When we meet another person, there they are, tending their own campfire.

When we decided to come together in the old form of relationships, we often had to choose which campfire we would sit at. The result was that one of us left our own fire unattended to eventually extinguish with neglect while we both piled logs of energy and attention into the dominant partner's campfire. Sooner or later, the person who had abandoned their campfire started to feel that something was missing from their life. Eventually, the neglected fire was going to need attention. Usually, this heralded the beginning of the end of this relationship.

In the incoming new relationships, we will discover that although we still start out with two separate fires, that by adding more wood and attention to them we can enlarge the scope of our campfires until the two fires merge into one large blazing bonfire of Love. We will create a campfire larger than either of us could make separately. And it's going to be easy since it has two devoted tenders!

Instead of looking at each other with concentrated attention to the exclusion of much else, we will be so deeply aligned within our One Heart, that we can both look outwards as two eyes of the same being. Thus shall we serve and nourish each other, while we are freed to serve others with the totality of our beings. Since we will be approaching these relationships from positions of wholeness instead of lack and neediness, we shall finally experience the fulfillment we have long sought.

As we progress along our journey towards Oneness, we will discover that the deep feeling of intimacy and ease of expression experienced in our closer relationships will be extended to an ever larger group of

people. For indeed, we are all Starry Family and soul mates to each other.

New forms of relationship are just being introduced. We have had to wait until we reached a certain level of Oneness within our own beings, until we had unified with our Divine Presence. Now we are ready to experience the joy of deep fulfillment, not only with our perfect partner and mate, but with our entire family of humanity!

To become whole total beings, we must welcome and embrace all parts of our being. This includes the unsavory aspects which we no longer need to fight or suppress. We simply love them into wholeness. By merging our shadows into our vaster Self, everything is transmuted into what is termed the *Great Light.*

It is important not to confuse the light and dark of duality with the Great Light. This Great Light is the union of all opposites into Oneness. It contains light and dark wedded together. It marks the completion of separation and denial, the ultimate transformation of duality. This is true spiritual alchemy!

When two are revealed to be One,
the veils of separation melt away and your natural state
of merged Essence into the One Heart is revealed.

You experience a total surrender as your entire being
opens to embrace the other into fullest union on dimension
after dimension until a *New* Octave of Oneness is reached.

Here you discover yourselves to be truly One with no
vestige of the illusion of separation remaining between
you. *Your* very cells and molecules have fused together.
Every breath you take is done in the wondrous unison of
One Breath.

Even what is perceived of as your separate forms, merely
serve as the Divine Mirror of the Oneness of your
combined being. They are the vehicles for the joyous
expression of your inherent Sacred Union.

No longer do you perceive of yourselves as individualized units of consciousness, for now your identity has become far vaster than either of you could achieve on your own.

The two pillars of fiery Light have fused into a radiant bonfire of One Heart which infuses all whom you encounter with a transcendent shaft of All Encompassing Love serving to further transform the many into the One.

Such is the form of service we have been Called forth to serve; that we have long yearned to embody. Our hearts Call us forth to beat as One Heart, to shine in our true form as one glorious Being of Love, purified in the sacred fires of Divine Bliss, reborn anew!

Sacred Union

Sexuality is a subject much talked about, but little understood.

This is one of the areas where duality has been most prevalent, although one of the main purposes of sex is to create union and Oneness. This duality manifests itself not only in the obvious one between male and female, but in the perceived separation between spirit and matter. This manifests in an irrevocable division between the upper and lower energy centers or chakras.

Many otherwise highly evolved people still equate sex and physicality with the lower chakras and spirituality with the upper ones. Even though most of the time they are attuned and open to the Higher frequency energies, when they become sexually stimulated their energies experience a shift to the lower chakras. Often this is felt as a real shifting of gears and shutting down of spiritual awareness. The opportunity for full expression of sacred union is lost while they turn to a level of animalistic gratification.

This is truly a pity, for there is such a universe of sacred expression, of fulfillment beyond your wildest dreams, waiting in the realms that have just been shut down. Although, on the physical plane sex takes place in the genitals and sexual organs, in reality, it is meant to be experienced throughout the entire physical, emotional, mental & spiritual bodies on multi-dimensional levels.

It is not my purpose here to delve into various sexual techniques. There are already numerous books available on this subject. Instead, I should like to explore a new way of approaching sexuality with our full beings.

This is making love as Angel with Angel, while consciously acknowledging that you are Shared Essence in the One Heart, two fragments of the One who are merging themselves back together with Love—uniting with open eyes and open hearts in dimension after dimension until you are carried back all the way home to the One.

First of all, you must do your inner work by aligning your own chakra system into one unified whole. Yogic breathing practices which circulate energy up and down your spine are most helpful.

You can begin at the base of your spine in the root chakra and slowly bring the breath up the spinal column to the second chakra, then up to the third and so on. Breathing with a slightly open mouth and upraised tongue is particularly effective. Do not try to force your breath to the top of your head all at once; this is not a race. Just go as far upwards as you can in a natural, relaxed pace. Then pause for as long as you can with ease; now slowly exhale.

Keep repeating this process until the energy finally reaches your crown. Breathe in from the root and move the breath upwards in the spinal column in steady increments. Along the way you might pause to give any needed healing to your chakras. When your energy moves smoothly from the base of your spine all the way to your seventh chakra, pause again, feeling the energy flow through you unifying your energy centers. Now breathe in three short breaths through your nose. Pause again, and you will have reached the state of No-Breath wherein you float within a sea of peaceful wholeness.

After you have healed any breaches within your own chakra system, then you are ready to begin unifying with another. Of course, if you pick a partner who has a huge internal wall between upper and lower chakras, it's going to be rather difficult. You're not going to meet with great success unless your partner really wants to experience full, *conscious* union through sex. Ideally, in order to do this you need a partner who has also unified their chakras. Angel with Angel, remember. It's also important that you have genuine love for each other.

There are no set rules for achieving this process. Your Angels can help you experience sacred union if you simply anchor their Presences inside you. But for the purpose of clarity, I will give you a possible example.

You can begin by sitting quietly facing each other while slipping in and out of meditation. Call in your full Angelic Presence. Look deeply into your partner's eyes seeing the Angel that they truly are, bathing in the pool of shared Essence. Drink deeply of your Angelic Presences while fully opening yourself to your partner.

Feel the energy flowing back and forth between your chakras, *all* your chakras. You may touch fingers lightly, sparking an increased flow of energy between you. Now follow the intuition of your Higher Self. You may begin to do mudras with your hands, regulating the energy currents or softly touch the other on their heart or forehead. All the while opening more of yourself, bringing in more of your vast Angelic Presence, merging your auras together in a swirling spiral of Golden Light.

If you wish, you may commence breathing together, moving your energies upwards from the base of your spine, aligning yourselves as One Being, chakra by chakra. Now your lips can touch, not in a kiss, but in a silent sealing of union. This is a highly sacred form of oral transmission.

You are now ready for the physical phase of love-making which can commence slowly and deeply.

Don't lose your focus on the One Heart which links you together in Oneness. As the lower energy centers ignite, move the sacred fire upwards to the crown chakra and beyond until all of you pulsates with electrical energy. Keep your entire beings aligned and engaged in this process. There is no hurry nor is there any need for orgasm, unless you desire it. Far more of you is uniting than ever before. It is often preferable to defer an orgasm, leaving yourselves in a state of heightened desire and merger. Then the next time, you can begin from this point and go ever further.

Whether you experience an orgasm or not, there will come a time when the energies have reached a certain pinnacle of heightened awareness. This is where most people think love-making is over. But it can be the starting point for a whole new octave of experience.

You can utilize these heightened energies to propel you to another dimensional awareness, going right into the Greater Reality.

Here you will discover the core of the One Heart which contains greater peace and union than you have ever experienced before. Together as One, you can fly freely within a state of sublime bliss into the Beyond.

Sometimes you may experience yourselves as two entwined Heavenly Beings whose transparent bodies are filled with stars, creating new starry galaxies through your love. Or you may simply melt into one vast sphere of Golden Light. Whatever form your sacred union takes, serves to bring you closer to our inherent state of Oneness. It is a doorway that few have chosen to enter, and even fewer have traveled to its destination.

First & Second Wave

Most of us belong to what we call the First and Second Wave.

If you are aligned with either the First or Second Wave, you will recognize yourself while reading the remainder of this segment.

The First Wave are those who came to Earth during the early colonization period from the stars. They are the ancient ones known as Gods and Goddesses who initially walked upon this planet in vast Light Bodies. In the beginning, they served in the task of co-creation, establishing the energy patterns which prepared for our subsequent descent into matter.

This new phase of immersion into matter entailed entering into a state of amnesia in which we forgot our Divine Origin and Purpose. We now walked upon the Earth in scaled down human forms weighted heavily by the density of gravity. Yet, there was still part of us who remembered the responsibility of the Higher Purpose we had chosen to carry throughout our cycle of incarnations. Always have we of the First Wave served as Pillars of Light. Working both publicly and behind the scenes, we have been instrumental in securely anchoring the Light and keeping the planet in rotational balance on its axis.

Some of the First Wave arrived after the descent into matter bringing with them useful talents and skills to aid humanity during its long passage through duality.

These are the ones whom ancient legends speak of as coming from the stars. They came here in order to trigger into full remembrance their starry brethren who had already undergone the step down into density.

The fully awakened First Wave could only remain on Earth in their full Presence for a time. Some of them left when Lemuria was ripped out of the magnetic grid. By the time Atlantis sank for the first time, coinciding with the disappearance of both AN and Shamballa from the physical plane, this signified a shift in frequency patterning which made it impossible to remain on the planet in their heightened state of consciousness. Thus many of the First Wave duly departed, returning to the starry realms. Others chose to remain and undergo the process of immersion into third dimensional density in order to continue their service to Earth.

Ever since then, the remaining First Wave have served here with dedication. Often their work has appeared to be unnoticed and unappreciated. Their experiences have been arduous and their sacrifices great. For much of their lengthy cycle of service, they labored under the illusion of being alone and cut off from the One. Their weighty responsibility has been a heavy burden for these very old souls.

I know about these things because I am of the First Wave. I remember, as do many of you. And in these accelerated times everything is in the process of great change. We now know that we are not serving here alone nor have we ever been. There is a vast group of us, both First and Second Wavers, who are joining together to awaken and activate humanity on a scale never before achieved. This is being done in the full Light of consciousness! What a supreme blessing for all of us.

It is now time for us of the First Wave to review our ancient commitments to the Earth.

We vowed to see the planet through to its time of ascension from duality, to irrevocably anchor Oneness. As this time fast approaches, it is imperative that we bring all facets of our lives to completion and fulfillment. Any areas which are still congealed in denial of our inherent Oneness must transform. We must acknowledge our Divine Heritage and Birthright.

Soon, we shall be asked to make our choice whether to return to the Celestial Realms and take on another level of service or to remain on Earth and join those of the Second Wave in building and establishing the New.

Those of the Second Wave entered this planet long after it was created and the etheric blueprint set into position. Their cycle of earthly embodiments is not nearly as long as that of the First Wave, hence they have less earthplane experience.

Much of their time away from this planet was spent on other planets and dimensional realms. They can be referred to as newer, younger souls, but this is merely in regard to Earth experiences, for Second Wavers have existed just as long as the First Wave. They have simply been gaining experiences away from the Earth.

The main function of the Second Wave is to establish the New Octave of Oneness upon Earth. They are the builders and manifestors of the new Divine Dispensation. They are not concerned with the anchoring of new energies, for that is the job of the First Wave. Thus many Second Wavers have been riddled with impatience and bristling with ideas for the creation of new forms of expression. They want to manifest now!

Unfortunately, there cannot be full expression of this creative potential until our transformation into Oneness is achieved. This is why it is imperative for First & Second Wave beings to work together at this time. Many First Wave are weary, having experienced a prolonged immersion into the third dimensional density. They need the fresh energy and optimism of the Second Wave in order to fulfill their cycle of service.

Interestingly enough, we often tend to choose those of the same wave as ourselves for friendships because there is a greater depth of understanding between us. In romantic relationships, the opposite is true. The union of First and Second Wave beings brings many needed gifts. The First Waver supplies the needed knowledge and wisdom of experience, while the Second Waver has a surplus of energy and enthusiasm.

As the members of the First Wave who choose to depart this planet shall begin leaving in 1992, culminating in their final removal at the end of 2011, it is imperative that those of the Second Wave activate quickly.

You need to rise up into your full authority and empowerment for the very pinions of this planet are being replaced. It's like a changing of the guard and you are the ones who must be ready to replace the First Waves who depart. A sceptre is being passed; if you are not in position to take it, who will be?

After this transition is complete, the real fun will commence. You will be able to openly create and manifest to your heart's content, fulfilling your Higher Purpose with dedicated abandon. This starry planet will ascend into Oneness, having served her original Purpose as a school for duality. Together, you shall rise as one radiant Being, spiraling into ever deeper, octaves of Light.

Starchildren

During this time of transition, we are experiencing an influx of new arrivals from the stars.

Many of them are coming in with their memories fully intact. Starchildren have been incarnating here in large numbers since the middle of the 1970s. For some this is their first Earth embodiment, but as yet, this is rather the exception. Most Starchildren have had earlier experiences here throughout the long course of history, but it has not been their primary field of manifestation. In between and often even during, their lifetimes on Earth, they are infused with direct linkage to their starry places of origin.

These unique beings are not part of either the First or Second Wave although they have come to aid them in the fulfillment of the Divine Plan for Earth. It is not necessary for them to partake in the struggles of duality; that does not serve their Purpose. Instead, they are surrounded with a forcefield of protection which maintains their innocence and integrity while on this planet. They are often born to awakened parents of the First Wave in order that these ones can supply the needed Earth experience. They are here to renew and reactivate our links to the stars.

Starchildren can be recognized by their great purity and innocence, with auras of deep wisdom and clarity, especially visible in their eyes which emanate a starry brightness. The younger ones have sweet, little budding wings.

Sometimes it is difficult when they have to go to third dimensional schools and interact with children of normal consciousness. We can serve Starchildren not only by sharing our knowledge and experience on the earthplane, but by opening ourselves to learn from the vastness of what they remember.

It benefits Starchildren greatly when we can take them to quiet places in nature and do not inundate them with too much television, although they are fascinated with it. Video games were created for these starry ones, which is why they enjoy such popularity. The accelerated action of these games closely resemble their star travels through the various galaxies, thus they can play them with rapt attention while renewing their star navigation skills.

Starchildren need time to be alone and quiet. They require utmost respect, strong love and gentle guidance. You may have difficulty trying to exert your parental authority with them since they are such empowered individuals. Yet, as they are children and newcomers to this planet, it is necessary that you do so when appropriate. It is important that you express your authority in as empowered a means as possible since

Starchildren will not tolerate willful domination. In parenting as in everything else, you will be much more effective if you emanate from your Angelic Presence. *Having five children of my own, two of whom are starchildren, I have learned this from my own experience.*

One of the most important things that we must do with our Starchildren is to bring them together with other Starchildren, regardless of age differences.

They have a great deal to share with each other, beginning with a profound recognition. It is essential that they know that they are not alone on this planet, and that there are many other Starchildren who *See* and understand. If they feel isolated and separate, it could be harmful and distressing to these beautiful beings.

I know that there are a few fine schools with a high consciousness already established for these children, but we need lots more of them. I am issuing the Call to some of you to create camps, gatherings, classes, books, magazines or whatever comes to you for these Starchildren. This is most needed for they are the seeds of our future. They need forms of creative expression, places where they can openly express what they know and remember, as well as opportunities to gather together with other Starchildren.

Empowerment

Empowerment is openly accepting and embodying that which you truly are.

It is the clear expression of your authority and is part of being an Angel. When you are empowered you emanate from your Highest Truth. This is not something that's thought about and planned out, it's simply a state of being in direct alignment with the One.

Since empowerment is the natural state of being ourselves, we might wonder why so many of us find it exceedingly difficult. This is due to some of our previous experiences with power during times past both on this planet and various other realms.

Many of the most conscious, highly capable beings on this planet are reticent to fully express their inherent power and Divine authority. They are still judging themselves harshly for some long ago misuse of power and are terrified of abusing power again. It is important to understand that each of us now incarnate has misused power at some time because that is part of the full spectrum of experience that comes with incarnating within duality. I'm not saying this to condone the abuse of power. We all experienced this in order to learn its effects. By now, many of us have learned this lesson well and have committed ourselves fully to serving the One.

We are not going to make that mistake again so we can quit judging ourselves and feeling guilty over how terrible we were long ago. This absolution of ourselves is essential so we can move forward as empowered instruments of Divine Intervention. The very survival of this planet and the life forms living upon it depends upon whether or not we can forgive ourselves for past transgressions and move forward as empowered beings.

We can stop being afraid of expressing our true power. We must stop defining power as domineering, arrogant, selfish, heartless behavior.

These are the adjectives which we have picked up from our past experiences during numerous embodiments. They no longer pertain nor did they ever accurately define power.

Our modern day dictionaries define power as: *l. The ability or capacity to do something. 2. A specific capacity, faculty or aptitude. 3. The ability to exercise authority. 4. Strength or force exerted or capable of being exerted. 5. Forcefulness, effectiveness.* None of those definitions sounds too frightening. In fact, true power is exactly what is needed for us to express today.

True power is simply energy, *empowered energy* which comes directly from the One. We came here to openly be ourselves, to serve the Higher Plan, not in a weak, wishy washy manner, but by expressing our Divine Heritage with authority.

It is good to be strong and empowered. Not in order to manipulate or control others, but to express the fullness of our Angelic Presence. Because we are not going to simply emanate power all by itself; this energy is going to be infused with love and wisdom. We're going to be *powerfully* loving and *powerfully* wise. We are going to powerfully serve to our fullest extent. Power is the force or strength or energy which is going to send forth our love and wisdom to ever greater distances. It is our method of propulsion. Without it, our love and wisdom will languish without full expression.

Lucifer & The Fallen Angels

This is a subject much open to misinterpretation and fear; yet, now is the time for Lucifer to be understood in the clarity of the Greater Light.

We must not only face our fears, but learn to embrace them in the All Encompassing Love of Oneness. There has been much written about Lucifer and the fallen Angels. There has also been a confusion of Satan with Lucifer although they were never referred to in the Bible as being the same person. This occurred at a later date. Since then, there has been a great deal of fear and apprehension attached to this subject. Now that we are awakening, it is time for us to look at this with a vaster perspective.

Long, long ago, Lucifer was found at the right hand of God as the brightest and most devoted of the Angels. His very name means *Bearer of Light*. To understand his story, we must go back in time to shortly after this planet was created. In those days, we walked openly upon Earth as Angels in Light Bodies with wings fully outstretched. Ancient legends from all over the world speak of the time when Angels walked upon the Earth. Others speak of giant races of God-like beings from the stars, were they not Angels too?

Come with me, dear ones,
Let us walk backwards
Through distant realms of time,
For we must remember.

Can you hear the Call?
Can you remember when you
Chose to remain and serve?
For that you did.

So great was your love,
So deep was your compassion,
So committed your dedication,
That you chose to answer the Call.

Please remember & acknowledge this.
You chose to serve upon planet Earth,
To play this drama to the end.
No one enticed you here.

You didn't come from unworthiness
Or because you had somehow failed.
You remained here out of Love.
As a fragment of the One.

The Descent into Matter

When the Call was sent forth asking for volunteers upon the Earth to aid in the transformation of matter, we responded by offering our services.

It was no longer possible for us to remain on Earth in our vast Angelic Bodies of Light. What was required was for our Angelic Self to send a small fragment of itself, a tiny starseed of its Essence, down to Earth on a Golden Beam of Light. This starseed was to interlock into matter. Hence we needed a method of propulsion to embed us into density. We had been thoroughly prepared for this process, at least as much as we could be, since it was beyond anything we had ever before experienced.

This is where Lucifer came in. Being the brightest of the Angels, he volunteered to take on the most difficult of tasks. This was the transmutation of the densest core of duality—that which was most separate from the One.

Lucifer served as the instrument to embed our starseeds deep within duality's third dimensional density.

This was experienced by us as a lethal blow, like a leaden dagger to the back of the neck, quite unexpected by us. When this happened, it caused us to feel for the very first time the emotions of shock, betrayal, abandonment, deep sorrow, anger and finally, guilt. Then we sank into forgetfulness. . . We forgot our Divine Origins. We forgot our Higher Purpose. We forgot that we were not separate from the One. Thus were we imprisoned in the matrix of duality.

Everything happened just like we had been told it would, only we hadn't quite believed it would be this terrible. Nothing in our previous state of limitlessness had prepared us for the rigors of the descent into matter. This is the time known as *The Fall.* Though, in truth, we fell not. It was merely part of the perfection of the Divine Plan.

At the moment when we descended fully into matter, we directed our new negative emotions towards Lucifer, for was he not the one who had caused us to suffer so! This too, was part of the perfection of the Divine Plan, for our combined negative feelings served as the method of propulsion to thrust Lucifer into the very core of density. This is where he had volunteered to serve with his Heavenly Legions who are now referred to as Fallen Angels.

They are the ones who offered to follow Lucifer into the density's core. Few of them have yet returned. Occasionally, I encounter some of the Fallen Angels who ever walk among us. They are usually resistant to my efforts to reawaken them, sometimes openly hostile, often hurriedly fleeing from my presence. I regard them with love and compassion for they have made their heavy journey of service into the corridors of darkness for all of us. I can feel their immense pain of separation and it saddens my heart. But until they are ready to return to Oneness, we can only embrace them in Love, waiting for their inevitable return.

And thus Lucifer and his legions of Fallen Angels have been locked into the core of duality, sealed within it by our collective fear and distrust which serves as the stone sealing shut their return to conscious Oneness.

Eventually, as we achieve our chosen task on planet Earth to transmute duality into Oneness, Lucifer and his fallen Angels must rise up into the Light to once again sit at the right hand of God as one of the brightest of the Angels. *For nothing and no one is separate from the One.* Within the Greater Reality, everything is of the One. So at some point in the not too distant future, we must embrace our fears of duality and love everything back into the radiant wholeness of the One.

The Legions of Archangel Mikael

The mighty Archangel Mikael has long served as the overseer and protector of our passage through the Template of Duality.

When Lucifer was put out of commission, so to speak, by volunteering to transmute the core of density, Mikael volunteered to take on the duties of watching over our evolutionary process. Thus has he served in this capacity since the descent into matter.

Those of us who entered the planet at that time are part of his Heavenly Legions. Some of the beings who incarnated at a later date are also united with him in Divine Allegiance. Thus we have a very deep connection with Archangel Mikael whether we have previously been aware of it or not, for we are bound with him in service to see this planet through its time of transition and ascension into the Template of Oneness.

Each of us who is in alliance with Mikael also carries his sword of Truth and Justice.

Many of us have carried it reluctantly throughout most of our unawakened embodiments. We could be seen dragging our swords upon the ground, not knowing what to do with them. Later on, during our awakening process when we were rift with inner conflicts, we often tried to deny our power and Divine given authority. Sometimes we attempted to throw away our swords; but somehow, they always returned to our side.

This was more of a problem than we realized at the time. When the weight of our sword of responsibility became too heavy to bear, we attempted to sabotage ourselves by plunging our swords deep into our bodies. Some of us still carry our swords imbedded within us, what I refer to as *the walking wounded*. If you are one, you will recognize it simply by reading these words. If so, you might now consider removing the sword of your power and Divine Heritage and begin the process of healing yourself. For you are needed here in all your full glory.

I have a dear, old friend, whom I have known throughout numerous incarnations, who has frequently assumed the role of a warrior, always fighting for noble causes. In times past, he has served to protect me and save my life, often at the expense of his own. Thus I have deep love and gratitude for him though I rarely see him. In this lifetime he is the holder of numerous high degree black belts in various martial arts and resembles a samurai, although he is American. The first time that I hugged him, I felt a hard object between us. On closer examination, I saw that it was a sword which stuck through his chest emerging out his back.

Initially, I assumed that it was left over from some old battle since most warriors still carry the psychic residue of conflicts they have experienced from many lifetimes of warring. Rarely do they allow themselves to be thoroughly healed. Also, it is not easy for them to find someone with the necessary skills and vision to heal them. I asked him if he was aware of the sword in his chest. He said that he had carried it for a long time. I knew that I could heal him, since for some reason, maybe lifetimes as a high priestess, I know how to heal warriors. So I asked for his permission to remove his sword at a more convenient time. This permission was readily granted.

I did not see him for many months, but one night I could not sleep and knew that it was time. I sat before my altar and went to an inner place. There I saw my friend with his sword. First I visualized the placement of two crystals at the sword's entry and exit points. This was in order to cauterize the wounds for I did not wish him to experience shock at the removal of what he had carried within him for so long. The crystals served to freeze those two points. Then I carefully removed the sword.

After I had done a great deal of healing in the places where the sword had been lodged, I turned my attention to the sword itself. It was quite bloody and disgusting. At first, I didn't know what to do with it. Then I realized with surprise, that it was his own sword which he had put inside his chest! He had wounded himself!

Next I saw Archangel Mikael standing above me patiently waiting for me to hand over the sword. This I did and Mikael held the sword up to his mighty sword. There was a flash of brilliant blue violet Light which instantly cleansed the years of conflict and bloodshed. Then Mikael returned the sword to my friend who vehemently did not want it back. Now the scene turned somewhat comical, as my friend repeatedly tried to throw away his sword. With all his great strength he hurled the sword as far away he could. In an instant, always did it return to his hand. Finally, he broke down and sobbed, for it could not be gotten rid of, in spite of all his efforts and will.

Over the next months, I checked in with my friend on

the inner planes. The wounds were healing well, but he still was fighting with his sword. Finally, there came that moment which I had long prayed for, in which acceptance was given and he stood tall, proudly brandishing his sword high to Heaven. He had accepted his power and responsibility.

It was almost a year later before I encountered my old warrior friend in the physical and there was a marked change in him. He was no longer fighting his internal conflicts and his life was beginning to smooth out. I told him of my experiences with his sword and he confirmed that he too, felt that it was finally gone and his ancient wounds had been healed.

The swords of Archangel Mikael cannot be turned in or exchanged until we complete what we have vowed to do here on Earth. First a purification must take place. For the past few years, Archangel Mikael has been recalling his swords in order to purify and renew them. As he recharges them with the full blue violet ray of his sword, all the nicks, scratches and spilt blood of past karma are removed.

They are as new again, just as they were when he gave them to us at the beginning of our cycle of embodiments. Then Mikael lovingly hands them back, for now the time has come for us to rise up into full empowerment. Not in order to join the many battles of duality currently playing out here and in the astral planes, but rather that we may rise victorious as one vast Legion of Light into realms of consciousness *beyond* duality. This is the true Final Battle. It is the end of war and separation. For the Legions of Archangel Mikael are being called Home.

First, we are being placed on Full Alert that we may reawaken from our long slumber, remember who we are, and step free of all levels of illusion. With our swords we will cut ourselves free from ignorance and regain our Divine Birthright and Heritage. We shall experience true completion of our Divine Mission. *And our Divine Mission is to consciously be that which we truly are!*

Like wings, the swords of Michael are excellent barometers of our present state of wholeness.

By observing your swords with your inner sight, you can ascertain how you are dealing with issues of power and authority. You might see yourself resting on the hilt of your sword when you are being contemplative, or brandishing it On High when you are feeling empowered. I have had some very interesting experiences viewing my own sword, as well as the swords of others. And some of us have the authority to activate and empower others with a strike of our sword against theirs. Sometimes, this facilitates a great awakening.

Of course, if the truth were to be told, you will discover that the Archangels are not separate from us. They represent our collective Angelness. When a large number of Angels gather together, we create and form the vast consciousness of an Archangel. Together we form the One. This is another instance in which the phrase, *"I am the One and the Many,"* has great significance.

This is similar to how the great beings on this planet have been created. Have you ever wondered why so many people have memories of being the same famous person from history? How could there be so many Nefertitis or St. Francis of Assisi? It's easy to assume that everyone is making it up, but maybe they're not. They feel that their memories are accurate. Perhaps, the great beings are formed by many units of consciousness joining together in one physical body. Possibly you *were* Nefertiti, but instead of being the entire person, you simply manifested as a hair on her head. But you were definitely a part of her; your memories are real. It is the state of linked souls which is mentioned in the Egyptian chapter of *The Legend of Altazar.* Maybe even now, each of us is a combination of numerous souls united together in order to experience the earthplane.

Although we perceive and address Archangel Mikael as a being separate from us, each of us resides within his vast being. We are more than a family, more than his Heavenly Legions, in truth, we are One.

The Archangels represent that part of us which has already attained a state of Divine Vastness.

I wrote this late at night. A few hours later while I was asleep, I heard the sound of several horses hooves approaching my house which is quite isolated. Next I heard a key turn in the front door and a man's footsteps come into my bedroom. This pulled me out of sleep and into fear. I forced opened my eyes and heavy with sleep said, "Who is there?" In the moonlight, I could see Archangel Mikael standing in my room. His body was beautifully delineated in White Light which outlined every detail of his robes and jeweled sword. He held a domed crown in his hand which he offered to me.

WE ARE ISSUING THE CALL
FOR THE LEGIONS OF ARCHANGEL MIKAEL
TO BE PLACED ON FULL ALERT.

NOW IS THE TIME
FOR YOU TO ACTIVATE,
FOR THE CALL TO ACTION
HAS SOUNDED.

THIS IS A FULL ALERT:
 ALPHA CODE FREQUENCY LINK UP:

THE LEGIONS OF ARCHANGEL MIKAEL
ARE CALLED TO REAWAKEN
AND STEP FORWARD
INTO FULL CONSCIOUS RECOGNITION
OF YOUR DIVINE MISSION AND PURPOSE.

THE LEGIONS ARE ON THE MARCH.
THE ACTIVATORS ARE AMONG YOU.
COME FORWARD THAT YOU MAY BE COUNTED.
CHOOSE YOURSELF AS AN INSTRUMENT
OF DIVINE INTERVENTION.

By Supreme Command of Archangel Mikael:

It has hereby been ordained by the Hierarchy of the Great Central Sun that the state of Divine Intervention currently in effect on planet Earth shall be intensified.

It is our intention that the Golden Ray of Divine Intervention be ever accelerated and stepped up in order to reawaken and reactivate humanity on a scale never before experienced.

It is an essential part of the Divine Plan that as many as possible receive empowerment as embodiments of multi-dimensional consciousness. This shall greatly aid and accelerate the process of the transition from third dimensional density into a state of multi-dimensionality.

Great shifts are called for in these momentous times. The choice is yours whether you prefer shifts of consciousness or geophysical shifts. If you choose to make the shift within your consciousness, it must be made now. There is no time to tarry. Hence you are being irradiated from On High with a constantly expanding, accelerating frequency in order to aid the restructurization process. Your Light Bodies are being prepared, for you shall don them soon.

Ahead of you looms an open doorway. This doorway must be passed through before you can experience the quantum leap into fully anchored, activated Oneness.

Anything that you hold onto which is anchored in duality shall prevent you from going through this open doorway. Thus this passage entails an absolute surrender of all parts of your being which emanate from your smaller self or ego.

A large measure of trust is also required. This will allow you to set aside your fears and make that great quantum leap through the doorway into the Unknown.

The choice is yours. The time is now. The future of this planet is in your hands.

We shall aid, encourage and support you in every way possible. We will shower you with blessings, protection and abundance. But first, you must make your decision to leap through the open doorway which stands in front of you. Thus may you serve as Instruments of Divine Intervention and conscious co-creators of the Divine Plan in action.

Archangel Mikael Speaks:

Beloved Ones of my heart & flesh, I Call you forth to remember and acknowledge your Divine empowerment and authority. We are well aware that these tumultuous times are difficult. Much is in play during these final days of the Time of Completion.

When you become impatient with the progress you have made, simply view it from the vantage point of eternity. What you are currently experiencing is the culmination of your entire cycle of earthly embodiments. Look at how far you have progressed in just a few brief years of time. Look clearly at how much you have achieved and released.

We have now reached the time for which you have long prepared. This is the fulfillment of our Divine Missions which each of us, singularly and as One, vowed to bring to its fullest completion. The time has come. Simply go deeply within your heart and allow yourself to remember. Go back to the time before we came to this planet when we rode through the Celestial Heavens as one, vast, triumphant Legion of Light.

Do you now remember hearing the Call sent forth on long Golden Trumpets to the farthest reaches of this dimensional universe? This Call was our signal to gather our forces together and descend to Earth. Each of us came here with a total commitment to the fulfillment of the Divine Plan. We carried no doubts or fears embedded within our cellular memory. These were accumulated during the long cycle of Earth incarnations. They have no place in our future endeavors.

Although it may appear that once we entered into the sphere of matter we were separated and dispersed, we were not. Whether in Heaven or on Earth, we ride as One. And thus it has been and always shall be.

We ride forth not to make battles, but as the victorious heralds of the One. As we bring forth and birth anew the Light of Oneness within our own hearts, thus shall we serve to transform the spheres of time, space & matter into ever increasing octaves of Love. We are here to foster unity, not the separation of duality. We are here to sow seeds of Love throughout the planet, illuminating all pockets of darkness until everything shimmers with magnificent, holy radiance. Remember that what is perceived as darkness or evil is merely a blockage of Light. For, in truth, there is only the Great Light. This state is reached by merging all polarities back into Oneness.

The ones here on this planet and in the astral realms who are consciously or unconsciously perpetrating darkness and discontent are all children of the One who have temporarily forgotten their Divine Origin and Heritage. They are merely playing out their appointed roles within the Template of Duality. Let us not be one of them! Sooner or later, all fragments of consciousness must return to the One Heart. We are serving here as one unified Legion of Light in order to awaken as many as possible.

In order to achieve this, each one of you is needed.

You are needed in a state of full empowerment and authority. You must have trust and confidence in yourself. You must cast aside any doubts and fears of your true magnificence as a Being of Light. Then please step forward in the fullness of your Presence. Together we shall love this planet awake. We will transform sadness into joy, hatred into love and struggle into abundance. This is what we came here to achieve. This is what we are Called to do. And the time is now.

Beloved Legions of Light, please bring out your swords and hold them High. I stand before you in my vast form of Blue Violet Light. Now, make your commitment to serving the Light anew. Open yourself to being a pure channel of the One. Feel the Light streaming down to you from Above. Let it penetrate your being—purifying and cleansing your spiritual, mental, emotional & physical bodies. Feel it dissolve the years of tears, the pain of separation, the veils of illusion and the fortresses of fear. Let Blue-Violet Light shower upon you and within you until you are reborn anew! Willingly release everything which has held you back and no longer serves your Highest Good, until you stand freely as a Pillar of Light!

As your swords are raised to the Heavens, I shall touch the tip of my sword to yours. A bolt of Blue Violet Lightning passes from me to you, traveling all the way down your sword into your arm, passing throughout your entire body in an instant. Thus have you received Activation and Empowerment. Now state three times:

I accept my Divine Heritage.
I accept my Authority.
I accept my Empowerment.
I accept my Responsibility.

Thus has it been ordained from On High by Supreme Command of Archangel Mikael, Lord of the Heavenly Hosts and the Council of the Elohim.

Now you have been purified and consecrated

To receive the Great Golden White Light

From the Great Central Sun.

The veils have been lifted,

The barriers dissolved,

So you may See and fully Be,

That which you truly are.

The Long Golden Trumpets

Are raised High once again,

And for the very first time,

The Call to Return issues forth

Across the Celestial Vastness.

The Stars

The Star That We Are

Back at the beginning, there was but one Star, the Star That We Are!

This magnificent Star is the Great Central Sun, a reflection of the One. Once we were all consciously united together within the fullness of our One Star. Merged fully, we experienced total, perfect union with the One.

After our Star imploded and exploded, what some refer to as the *Big Bang*, we separated into tiny fragments of Star. Thus the sky filled with myriad stars  which were but parts of the same Star. Many spirits clustered together into one starry fragment. These are the ones whom we now term soul mates.

1.

When our starry fragments could become no smaller, we underwent another transformation, this time into individualized units of consciousness which are called

Golden Solar Angels, although in truth, we never separated from the One. For these Golden Angels can also be viewed as Golden Rays or Beams of Light emanating from the One.

When the Call came to descend into matter in order to aid in the transmutation of duality, we, as Golden Angels, chose to answer the Call. However, it was not necessary for us to descend into the third density with

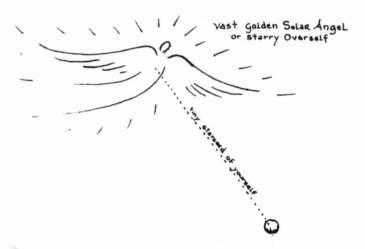

vast golden Solar Angel or Starry Overself

tiny starseed of yourself

our full Presence. All that we had to do was to send a small shaft of Golden Light earthward and anchor it therein. This shaft of Light was like a tiny Golden Beam or Ray of Light from our Star of One. It was a holographic projection from the vastness of our Starry Overselves.

This minuscule starseed of our true greatness was the part of us which embedded itself into matter. This is the tiny part of ourselves who has lived out the cycle of repeated incarnations on planet Earth.

At first, we were well aware of our true origin. We remembered that we were vast, starry Angels ever residing in the Celestial Realms and that only a small part of our total beings was involved in the earthly experience. This gave us great freedom as well as unlimited access to tremendous wisdom and grace.

But then our memories started to dim. We began to take life on planet Earth seriously, so seriously that we thought that it was the only reality. We forgot who we truly are. We started to feel separate from the One. At this point we had reached the position of anchoring our consciousness solely at the tip of the Golden Ray of our Star. Instead of facing inwards towards the center of our Star and remembering that we had never separated from the One, we turned our gazes outward into the empty void. *No wonder we felt lonely and cut off!* This is how it was for us living life in the third dimension. We felt homesick and alone, ever filled with sorrow and despair, as an un- requited yearn-

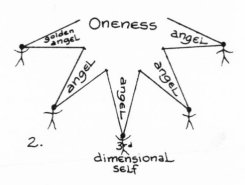

ing gripped our souls for perfect, fullest union / reunion with the One.

Thus was the pattern established for our numerous embodiments on Earth. Always searching for union, while unable to see that we have never separated from the One.

Our endless journey took us in one large spiral and this entire spiral was always within the body of the One. You could say that the map of our journey is merely the shift from unconscious to conscious Oneness. For in truth, we never left Home. Although it certainly appeared that we did as long as we identified with ourselves as stranded, separate tips of rays of Star.

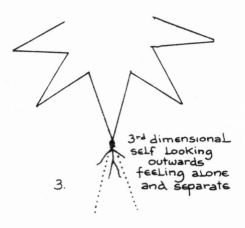

3.

3ʳᵈ dimensional self looking outwards feeling alone and separate

Now as we reawaken and remember who and what we truly are, we embark upon the journey homeward. This entails retracing our footprints back Home. We were birthed from the One Star into myriad stars, then as fragments of stars we transformed into Golden, Solar Angels in the Celestial Realms. These Angels sent earthward their Golden Shafts of Light which embedded starseeds into the planet creating humans. Now we must reverse the process. First we must turn around, facing back into the center of our Star, and remember that we are already whole and complete, always united in Oneness.

This step alone represents a massive quantum leap for humanity. It signals the beginning of a new phase of wholeness and freedom. It heralds awakened humanity's graduation into Mastery. It allows you to complete yourself within the Template of Duality so you may move onto the New Octave of Oneness.

This brings the entrance of the Golden, Solar Angels! Remember that these magnificent starry beings are you. They are the vast part of yourself who remained Home. They are the Golden Rays of our glorious Star. Once you contact your Golden Angel and bring its Presence deep inside, you are free to travel up the Golden Ray back to Source. You are loosened from the confines of duality. *This means that duality is no longer your predominant reality.*

You gain an ever greater ease in moving through time, space and matter while becoming increasingly receptive to that which originates from the realms of the Unseen. You begin to see far more than you could with your physical eyes, hear more than with your physical ears, etc. You are no longer limited to experience what is perceived as the third dimensional reality.

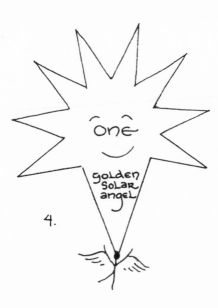

As you travel ever upwards on the radiant Golden Ray which leads back to the center of our Star, you enter the Zone of Merged Essence where many rays have overlapped. This is the territory of the Archangels, for they represent the unified consciousness of vast legions of Angels. They are not entities separate from us, but symbolize that part of us which has already attained a state of vastness. Right now there are beings serving upon this planet who emanate an Archangelic awareness. Although they incarnate in one physical body, they can no longer be perceived as being simply one individual consciousness, for they have already united with a larger portion of themselves.

And this is the journey that all of us shall travel on our accelerated path Homeward!

I Am Solaris Antari.

Above you is the Golden, White Star
Emanating from it are Golden Rays
These radiant starbursts of Light
Shower down upon you
Casting Golden Sparks of Illumination
Throughout your entire being.
They are the agents of quickening.

Before you are strands
Of shimmering Golden Light
Rippling with charged currents
This is the path for you to follow.
I shall joyously be your guide
Leading you from heart's pure core
Through destiny's completion
To reunion with the One Heart.

Onward we shall proceed
Into the fullness of Light
Bringing yearning's fulfillment
Into the ever perfect present.
Breathe in deeply this Golden hue,
Let it merge within your cells
Until you, yourself, are the Golden One.

Within you shall discover
What you always have been,
What, united, we are.
The Angelic Presence embodied,
A fragment of the One Star.

Star Alignments

Being in direct vertical alignment with our Star is the key to remaining balanced and empowered.

Thus it is important to maintain remembrance of the Great, Golden White Star which is always directly overhead. As long as we stay in its Golden Beam we are in direct alignment with the One.

Often we forget its radiant Presence and lose our sense of relatedness to the One. This is when we become unbalanced by discordant energies around us and pulled back into duality as our heightened perspective is temporarily lost.

Therefore it is of utmost importance to maintain your contact with the Star That We Are, always above you. Test this out for yourself the next time that you are drawn away from your Angelic Presence. As soon as you recognize the state that you are in, simply remember the Star and breathe in its Golden Light. You will feel an immediate sense of balance and calm peace reentering your being.

We have a wonderful process called Star Alignments where we reconnect with our Star and eventually merge with it. This process strongly aligns our Light Body with our physical body.

After we have merged into our vaster being, we walk around and randomly encounter one another, recognizing that we are all fragments of the same Star. It is an inspiring and powerful experience.

If you wish to do this at home or with a group of friends, you will experience some tremendous results. We have an excellent tape available of the Star Alignment process.

Right now you can try it out if you wish. You may play some beautiful music while you are star aligning to heighten the energies. Then stand up and claim your space. Think vertically and feel yourself as a radiant, free standing Pillar of Light. If you are doing this with a group of people, stand in a circle, giving yourselves lots of room. You might want to first stretch and move your body to feel its aliveness.

Now breathe in deeply and while you breathe out release your cares and worries. As you breathe, you can turn your attention to the Star above you, feeling it activate. As it becomes ever more radiant, it showers you with waves upon waves of Golden Light. Feel the Golden Light surround you and melt into the ground. Continue to breathe in Golden Light from the Star above you. Let this Light fill your being. Gently breathe out mists of Golden Light.

Next, you are going to reach up towards the Star and as you do, the Star is going to slowly emit a sphere of Golden Light which is going to gently land in your outstretched hands. Bring this sphere of Golden Light to rest upon the top of your head. Here it is going to open up into a magnificent Golden Crown.

This Crown belongs only to you and symbolizes your Divine Birthright and Heritage. Feel the Golden Crown upon your head and let yourself experience a sense of heightened empowerment. Look closely at your Crown, noticing the details of what it looks like. Get its image so clear in your mind that you could draw a picture of it.

Now you are going to reach up towards the Star once again. This time you are going to direct downwards a stream of liquid, crystalline Light which contains within it thousands of tiny Golden Stars. This star-filled liquid Light is going to enter your body from the center of your Crown. Bring this starry Light inside your head and feel those tiny Stars healing and reactivating you.

Breathe in yet more liquid starry Light and fill your neck with it, paying particular attention to the back of your neck where the unresolved sorrows of the heart tend to gather.

Then you are going to call in more crystalline, liquid Light filled with tiny Golden Stars, moving them down through your head and neck across your left shoulder into your left arm. Bring the Light all the way into your fingertips on your left hand. Feel your left arm filled with Starlight. Now let's repeat the process into the right side. Breathing in from the Star overhead, through your head and neck across the right shoulder, down your arms to the fingertips. If you want to scan yourself, you might notice that your arms feel a lot lighter and longer than the rest of your body!

Pause for a minute before you resume breathing in crystalline, starry Light from your Star. Bring it down to your upper torso, traveling all the way to your waist. Fill that area with tiny Golden Stars. Breathe in a special concentration of Stars to your heart area. Here you will feel the Stars transform into an exquisitely beautiful Golden Flower. This Flower unfolds its petals and expands within you into its full radiance.

Let's resume bringing in more liquid starry Light; this time filling your abdomen, buttocks, internal organs, all the way to the root chakra. Pay particular attention to any areas which have health problems or which you tend to ignore. By now you should be feeling as if you have an expanded body filled with Light, standing on very short, stocky, heavy legs!

So we're going to bring in Light from our Star down to the left leg, running it through the thigh, knee, lower leg, ankle and into the tip of every toe on your left foot. It's important not to forget any of your toes, each of them wants to be filled with Golden Stars. Now scan again, doesn't your right leg feel shorter and heavier than the rest of you! In fact, it may be difficult to make your legs feel like they are the same length.

Return yet again to the Star ever above you and breathe in more crystalline starry Light, sending it down your right leg, all the way to the tips of every toe on your right foot. Now, don't you feel different—a lot lighter and larger?

Well, we're not done yet. Let's bring in another concentrated sphere of tiny Golden Stars and put them in the center of our back, right between our shoulder blades. This is our wing area and we're going to give our wings permission to open and expand. Breathe into the Golden Stars inside your back and breathe out your wings, allowing them to fully unfurl. Doesn't that feel wonderful! Notice your newly found sense of balance, now that your wings are open. Feel the freedom of your open wings!

One last thing you can do is to scan your body again and see if there are any hidden pockets of distress, unexpressed emotions or physical problems which need extra healing. Do you have any places where your Stars are sort of skimpy? If so, simply reach up to the Golden Star ever above and breathe in more crystalline, liquid starry Light and place it where it is needed. Remember that your Star has an unlimited supply, so you don't need to be frugal with them. You can always return to the One for more. Anytime day or night, your Golden White Star above you is open twenty four hours and you don't even need a plastic card! We only have to remember that it's there and remain in direct alignment with it.

Now that we have activated our Light Bodies and strengthened our connection with the One, there's a lot more we can do. Some of the group work is on my *Star Alignment* tape. If you haven't heard it yet, you will just have to follow your own inner guidance which is what this Star-Borne work is all about.

One of the most profound things you can do after you have anchored your Light Body is to receive your personal mudra. This is a simple gesture or series of gestures, done with the hands and arms which represent your unique personal expression of the One. Do this gesture several times, until you do it with ease and will not forget it. Notice how good it feels. Feel the strength that it gives you. Our mudras are extremely powerful tools for keeping aligned with our Golden White Star and anchoring our Angelic Presence.

During daily life you can utilize your mudra much like your Angelic Name. Each time that you use it *(and you can be subtle about it, if you wish)* you will be strengthening your Angelic Presence. I use mine a lot, usually in an abbreviated form. I was watching a videotape of a television program that I was on and I must have used the short form of my mudra twenty or thirty times! *(It was an hour show.)* Most people simply thought I was making a hand gesture, but my Angelic friends laughed when they recognized my mudra. It certainly helped to anchor my Presence. Try it and you'll see what I mean.

Here's another thing you can do if you are in a group of people standing in a circle. After bringing in the Light from your Star like we just did, open your eyes and to the accompaniment of music, walk around and greet each other as shared Essence or as Angel to Angel. Do not allow yourselves to talk or touch each other, or else people often fall into their old patterns of relating. You may acknowledge each other with your mudras if you wish. This is a wondrously powerful experience. After doing it, you will never relate to each other again as just third dimensional personalities.

This is simply a small taste of the immense world opened up to us by doing Star Alignments. Feel free to discover many new wonderful ways of relating to one another. For this process helps us return to our natural state of Oneness.

Star Lineages

Star Lineages represent our starry genealogy on our path back to Source.

They delineate which Golden Ray of our radiant Star of Oneness we emanate from. This is similar to earthplane surnames since they reflect our family tree, or in this case, Golden Ray of Star. Star Lineage names refer to the *Zone of Merged Essence* within the Golden Ray, hence they are shared with many.

Within this Zone of Merged Essence is a *Zone of Overlap* where many individual rays unite. Each Zone of Overlap represents a different star lineage. They also denote a stage of fragmenting long ago when we were fragments of stars after our Star collapsed. Thus those with whom you share a common star lineage are the same ones with whom you traveled as fragments of star, for that was the first stage in the formation of star lineages.

Your Angelic Names contain the clues to your star lineages.

We almost always have more than one Zone of Overlap. Imagine if you will, a star with rays much like a flower with multiple petals, each of which overlap.

You can see on a flower that one petal will overlap with at least two other petals, one on each side. With a non-linear star which is multi-faceted, there are emanations of light protruding in all directions, not just around what we perceive linearly as the outer circumference. These rays overlap other rays, not just on each side, but on top and bottom as well. And that's only a simplification; it's actually more complex.

Remember that each overlap represents a Zone of Merged Essence. Each Zone of Merged Essence represents a former merger with a star fragment aeons ago. Whether you are following this or not, by now you might be wondering just what use is this rather obscure piece of esoteric information?

The Higher Purpose is our chosen task of returning Home to ever greater Oneness. This is achieved by reuniting our star fragments, recreating our original state of Oneness! To reunite our Star, we must begin with what is smallest and closest to us and proceed from there. To retrace our footprints back Home we first remember how we arrived here. This process has already begun by reuniting with our Golden Solar Angels.

Now what were we before we became Angels with individualized units of consciousness? We were tiny star fragments. But even in our smallest form as starry fragments, we were always linked with our Starry Family in the One Heart.

To ascend the stairway to the stars, we reunite our star fragments, bringing our Starry Families into ever larger groups of Oneness. When everyone realizes their inherent Oneness, we are Home!

We have glued back together our Star, *the Star That We Are*. And of course, the glue that we use is Love.

Reclaiming our star lineages is an important step on the journey Home. That's why it's so beneficial for us to come together and birth our Unified Presence!

To use myself as an example, I have two easily recognizable and quite common, star lineages. One is the Solara. Not only are there other Solaras, but my lineage would include all Solanas, Solas, Solayus etc. The Antara lineage is also proving to be quite extensive. This would include all variations on Antara including Antar, Antarion, An etc. Someone with the name of Itar would overlap lineage with an Antar, and an Istar would share a lineage with Itar and Antar. As I've stated before, there's a great deal to be learned from our Angelic Names.

At our workshops we have discovered many new star lineages. That's one of the reasons I love getting you all together; we have much to learn from each other. We are truly pioneers into new frontiers of the Unknown.

For those of you who have read my book, *The Legend of Altazar* and found recognition of yourselves in the characters therein, I'll let you in on a secret. The names of these characters represent various star lineages and archetypes of humanity. Not surprisingly, many people including some who have *not* read the book, have discovered these archetypes to be part of their Angelic Names.

Our Angelic Names represent our star lineages which are our direct pathway back Home. Let's travel together and make our return to the One.

The Fourth Dimension

As we attain our freedom from the third dimensional confines of time / space, we begin to enter what is termed the fourth dimension.

Much has been said about this dimension, but little is correctly understood. The fourth dimension was fully birthed and anchored into the Earth during the Harmonic Convergence on August 16th & 17th, 1987. The significance of the fourth density is that it is *the doorway* to multiple dimensions. This means that once your consciousness enters the fourth dimensional octave that you have access to multi-dimensionality. The fourth dimension is *not* to be lingered in, for of itself, it is not that important or exalted a place to be.

As it is the home of the astral plane, one will find rampant illusion present within the fourth dimension.

This is where many seekers have gotten stuck in the worlds of glamourous illusion. Many who entered the realms of spirituality through the use of drugs have found themselves mired in fourth dimensional, astral delusion. These are the spheres of both gods and demons—duality played out with enhanced drama and magic.

Some of you may have opened this door with the early experiments with psychedelic drugs in the late 1960s. These drugs were made widely available on this planet during that time in order to affect an accelerated shift in consciousness, although they also caused a high rate of attrition as many people were unable to handle the rapid changeover in awareness without suffering severe harm. Many were lost to insanity, drug addiction, weird religious cults and even death. Numerous others who suffered severe damage to their auric bodies, losing mental clarity and vital energy, required years of healing.

It was a fast road through the astral realms of illusion, laced with just enough spiritual revelations to awaken those whom survived this process that they might alter the collective unconscious of planet Earth to receive higher frequency vibrations due to be introduced on Earth during the 1980s.

The 1960s flung open the doors to the fourth dimension which was rife with both delusion and inspiration; the 1970s served to ground our newly expanded awareness, while the 1980s moved our level of consciousness to a more refined accelerated frequency, anchoring the fifth dimension. And during the 1990s the Greater Reality will be revealed. What a journey we have been through!

A Tale of Two Brothers

Many years ago I lived in London. This was during the famous *hippie* days, which in England played itself out with great fantasy. Young men and women dressed colorfully in velvets and silks like characters from a medieval play. It was a most creative time for the arts, especially music, which surged forth with inspiration, dissolving previous boundaries. We were seekers searching for the meaning of life, delving quickly into astrology, Tarot, *I Ching*, numerology, Buddhism, Hinduism and anything else we encountered.

Our previously drab lives had suddenly been transformed into magic. Old rules and morality were thrown away as we relished our newly discovered freedom to find out who we were. We went about in large groups of friends, feeling a strong bond of family with whomever we encountered. In many ways, it was a magical and idyllic time; unfortunately, it was also rampant with illusion.

During this period, I had a friend who was a young, struggling musician (*many of the people I knew were*), whom I shall call Colin although that was not his real name. He was a beautiful young man with long blond, curly hair and clear blue eyes. Colin came from a family who belonged to one of the secret esoteric schools in England. He was a very aware, pure being. Since he lived nearby, we visited with each other often—sharing our latest spiritual discoveries, listening to demo tapes from his recording sessions and encouraging each other.

One day he arrived rather distraught about his younger brother Mick, whom I had never met. This brother was a student at Cambridge who had recently returned from a trip to India. He had just been placed in a mental ward. Colin explained that Mick's journey had begun to go strangely when he was traveling through Yugoslavia and had joined up with a student from there who was also on his way to India. The two students discovered that their birthdays were one day apart in the same year.

When they arrived in India, they were met at their first stop by a Swami who greeted them profusely, stating that one of them was the Antichrist, the other one, an impostor. Neither of them knew what to make of this. Yet, it was not an isolated occurrence. Several times during their travels in India did they meet Swamis who seemed to recognize them. They were told many predictions of their future during this time.

After Mick returned to England, the predictions began to unfold, exactly as foretold. The last one had said that he would end up in a metal cage, which was where he now found himself. Colin asked if I would be willing to meet with Mick when he was released from the hospital, to see if I could help him. And of course, I agreed.

Some weeks later, Mick arrived at my small flat. His appearance was a total surprise. Where Colin was blonde and radiating Light, Mick was an absolute contrast, with black, straight hair, dark brown eyes and totally different energy. It was hard to see that they were remotely related at all, much less brothers. However, I resolved to try to help him.

After talking to Mick for a short while about his

experiences, it became apparent that he actually wanted to be the Antichrist! This was not what I had expected. I felt exceedingly uncomfortable in his presence and kept our visit as brief as possible.

The next time I saw Colin, I told him what I had discovered and that there was no way to help Mick unless he wanted help. Colin mentioned that his brother had taken to wearing a long, black top coat and stovepipe hat and had recently jumped off the roof of his building. Miraculously, he survived with minor injuries.

I spoke to Colin of duality and the perils of polarization. I could see that Mick carried deep resentment for Colin and his Light and would probably try to destroy him at some point. The most important thing was that Colin stay in his own energy field. And although it sounded weird at the time, I warned Colin never to get drawn into thinking that he was the Christ, for that was how I felt the polarization would manifest itself. It's just like a chess match between dark and light, whenever you get pulled onto the board, you open yourself up to being checkmated. Colin listened carefully and incredulously stated that he could never think of himself as the Christ.

Many months later I left London and moved to a remote cottage in the middle of Wales. Late one stormy night in the midst of howling gusts of wind, there was a mighty pounding at the door. Opening it, there was Colin standing uninvited. His hair was matted and his eyes were wild. He had just spent a week in some cave in the mountains. There he had experienced a major revelation that he was the Christ! And he felt he should find us and tell us.

Poor Colin, there was nothing I could do for him. I tried explaining that we are all the Christ, but it didn't get through. He stayed with us for a day or two, but he was now a stranger. Looking into his eyes, there was nobody there to recognize.

It's almost the end of this story and I'm sorry that I can't neatly resolve it for you. I saw Colin but one more time. It was a year or two later on the streets of London. I didn't recognize him until he spoke to me. There he was with a shaved head wearing the robes of the Hari Krishna sect selling magazines on the street. He still believed that he was the Christ. And I have not seen or heard of him or his brother since that faraway day, but sometimes in moments like this one, I wonder what happened to them. Are they still lost in the web of polarization and duality?

I share this story with you for one main purpose. Each of us can encounter someone who has the potential to polarize us, to checkmate us off our chosen path of destiny. Someone may come to mind for you right away, perhaps it is an old relationship or some member of your family. When and if you do encounter this person, it is important that you do not let them intrude within your sphere and that you do not give your power away. Because if you do, you shall be locked into duality with them until you are wise enough to reclaim your freedom. This is one of the traps of the world of duality that you might wish to avoid, for it is much easier to remain free of it at the beginning, than to free yourself later.

The Fourth Dimension Continued

In the astral worlds, one also finds the intergalactic warriors, ever dueling to save and destroy planets as well as entire star systems.

They are among us today, still battling and wagering over the fate of worlds, continuing their fight throughout myriad dimensions. Many of them are presently physically incarnate. They are learning about the issues of power and control whether the battles be played out on the magnetic grid, stargates, or states of consciousness. Most of these inter-galactic warriors were involved in Atlantis with similar issues. Their lesson continues.

Their ships can be seen in our skies as lower density manifestations than the ships of Light. Forever fighting with their own shadowed reflections, always requiring an outside *enemy* in order to avoid looking within, these are the realms in which warriors are eternally bound until they choose to lay aside the sword and embrace the One. The battle with duality can never be won, only fought over and over, endlessly. Sometimes winning, sometimes losing, but never experiencing final resolution until the entire concept of duality and separation is set aside. Many are those who confuse fourth dimensional delusions with spiritual reality, becoming seduced by the drama of ego's self importance and the glorious excitement of spiritual warfare which are always based on the premise that one side is right, the other wrong.

Some of the ones among us now carry memories of destroying their home planets, usually through terrible accidents or cosmic catastrophes.

They are here either to atone for their tragic misdeeds by helping to preserve this planet or they are the prophets of *doom & gloom*, feeding thoughtforms of scarcity and lack. You will often find these ones hidden away in their bomb shelters with arsenals of weapons and stored foods for the hard times to come. Never having healed the intensity of the trauma they have experienced, they tend to justify the destruction of planets as a necessary step of evolution. These attitudes are fueled by immense layers of guilt which are no longer necessary as a motivation in our lives.

Here also you can find the game plan for the Battle of Armageddon.

Right now, both sides are putting on their armor and preparing for the war which has already begun. On this planet we can clearly see the lines forming. We have Moslem against Moslem, Moslem against Christian, Communist versus Capitalist, haves against have nots, Israelis against Arabs, Fundamentalist versus New Age, and on and on, each perceiving the other as the personification of the AntiChrist.

It's as if a giant chess board was all set up with the pieces in their correct positions, waiting with ready anticipation for the game to begin. The War of Armageddon can and will play itself out, *if* we choose to participate. But what if we don't? What if enough of us raise our consciousnesses to a Greater Reality which is *beyond* the sphere of duality. Then maybe, there will be no terrible battles and the AntiChrist will not need to manifest. There will not be enough of us who focus our attention on these things, giving them power and life. As it was aptly said in the 1960s, *"What if we gave a war and no one showed up?"* It simply couldn't play itself out! *Remember that energy follows thought.* Where there's no energy or thought, there is no manifested reality. Maybe we could use our energy to create something more inspiring. Isn't that what we came here to do?

**Earth received a new etheric blueprint
during Earth Link on February 13th & 14th,
1988 when a shaft of brilliant blue violet
Light penetrated through Ayers Rock or
Uluru, in Central Australia and lodged in the
crystal beds beneath it.**

This new etheric blueprint has established a
recalibrated foundation enabling us to finally anchor
Oneness. That is why the old prophecies of *doom and
gloom* such as those of Nostradamus, no longer pertain;
they are the prophecies of duality. *We are now under
a new Divine Dispensation.* We are here to ensure
that the Earth experiences a gentle transition from the
old Template of Duality into the new Template of
Oneness. And once Oneness is truly anchored, we are
here to birth a new paradigm of Love. In order to serve
as midwives for our planet's ascension, we must first
birth the new paradigm of Oneness within ourselves.

Please be aware to choose with careful discernment just where you put your energy. Ask yourself:

· Am I sowing seeds of fear and separation or
seeds of clarity, love and Oneness?

· What parts of myself do I nourish and honor?

· Which voice do I listen to? The distorted voice of
my fears and doubts or the authority of my
Higher Self?

· Do I spend my time in the company of people
who encourage and uplift my Highest Truth or
with those who put me down?

· What fears or sense of unworthiness cause me
to shut myself down or make myself smaller?

It's your choice where you place your energy, and if you choose anything less than the fullest expression of your Highest Truth, then you might want to examine why.

We become what we put our attention into. Just imagine what will happen when you accept the fact that you are a Starry, Angelic Being, *consciously* serving here on Earth.

The door will open into an entirely New Octave of All Encompassing Love! This New Octave of abundance and fulfillment has been here all along, waiting for us to awaken and rise beyond the confinement of duality. Why not dare to be courageous and allow yourself to be fulfilled and happy, right here, right now, while we're in human embodiment. It's not so hard to accept once you get used to it. Even your physical being recalibrates itself in order to integrate the heightened frequencies of Love.

Star Beings

There is a major difference between what we term *star* energies and *space* energies. Star energies emanate from higher dimensional realms of Light, far beyond the illusion of duality.

Star beings form concentrated Light Bodies when they wish to be perceived by us. Their true form is diffused Light Essence. Star beings do not need or desire to physically incarnate on this planet. They have chosen to remain in heightened frequencies of awareness in order to serve on a much greater scale than can presently be imagined.

There are myriad orders of Starry Brotherhoods existing in the cave heavens on higher frequency octaves.

These cave heavens can be perceived as egg-shaped bubbles in space. Ancient traditions as varied as the Buddhist, Taoist, Inca & Hopi, tell of the existence of starry beings within their legends and prophecies. As Star-Borne, we are linked to these Starry Brotherhoods in deep kinship. They are as a family to us.

One of these is the *Brethren of the Og-Min* which I have mentioned in my previous books. *Og-Min* is a Tibetan word translated as *No-Down, No-Return*. This means that having reached their current level of starry consciousness, there's no longer any need to incarnate into physical worlds, unless they so choose. On the rare occasions that this happens, they would be considered a

Bodhisattva, one who has incarnated out of deep compassion to serve in humanity's enlightenment and liberation from duality.

The *Og-Min* are particularly significant because they are the Keepers of the Grid in charge of the Golden Beam which keeps this galaxy in positional alignment. There are several levels of attainment within their starry orders. The first level is found within the Halls of Og-Min, great caverns filled with banks of white candles. Long, low chanting fills the air, as white robed figures sit in silent devotion.

The intermediate level is discovered within smaller caves with large windows overlooking the starry sky. Here are fewer beings who are quieter still. Their teachings are no longer given in words or transmissions, but in direct, personal experiences which transform. To enter the advanced levels of the Og-Min, we must undergo numerous initiatory experiences wherein our beings are liberated from all previous boundaries and limitations. When this is achieved, you become an Og-Min incarnate.

Star beings do not travel in starships. They reside in simultaneous dimensions which exist outside of and beyond the time / space continuum.

Once we have made the connection with our starry brethren, we can enter their spheres at will, for part of us ever resides there. Please remember that star beings do not need to incarnate, walk-in, or arrive in space ships in order to contact us. Most importantly, they are never frightening or threatening. They are ever present within an expanded awareness and can be freely accessed whenever we align with their frequency level. Their connection with us serves to further recalibrate our beings.

Voyage on the Celestial Barge

I found myself in a small cavern of the Og-Min. This was part of the intermediate levels which I had been visiting since my initiation in the Grand Tetons a year ago. There was a large oval window set into the curves of the cave which looked out upon a vast starry sky. The Golden Beam passed vertically through this room, shimmering and rotating in position.

Xeron stood before me. He/she is one of the Og-Min whom I have been visiting with for the past six years, a most profound and loving teacher for me. A sphere of brilliant white Light emanates from Xeron's head and each of its outstretched hands.

I feel so battle weary and worn out, tired & grim. As I gaze at Xeron, he/she becomes the three spheres of Light. It is all I can see anymore. Then lines of Light like neon strands, link the spheres into a radiating triangle of Light. All else is in darkness. I realize that I am to step through this doorway created by the triangle.

As I pass through, I find myself in open space full of

stars. I feel as if I'm falling, but I'm not. It's more like floating. I feel cradled by the ceaseless rhythms of undulating star waves. This is most soothing, gently floating upon the starry currents. I hear music, deep Celestial resonances that calm my troubled being.

Rocking gently to and fro as if on a raft, I discover that I am in a heavenly boat, long and narrow, with gracefully upturned ends. It is a Celestial Barge, so elegant and Golden, sparkling and shimmering like a cluster of stars.

I am reclining on magenta silk cushions, nestled deeply in layers of soft pillows, floating gently through the sky. Briefly I wonder as to my destination, but then let go of thoughts and simply enjoy my journey.

I am so comfortable that I quickly fall asleep, sleeping deeply. While I am asleep, Golden Angels come, bending over me in loving concern. They sing to me sweetly, caressing me with waves of All Encompassing Love. Singing to me the songs of stars. That which I had long forgotten. And since I am lightly clad, they cover me with a simple cloth of white, protecting me against the chill of night.

Their songs soothe my tired soul, reminding me of octaves of harmony that have long been distant. So far away had I traveled from Home. Layers of the harshness and brutality accumulated during the rigors of everyday existence begin to dissolve.

I feel cool hands smoothing my aura, healing the nicks and bruises with wave upon wave of Golden Love.

So long have I yearned to be held and soothed. So long has my being cried out for gentleness and purity. What have I done to myself to keep myself here? The world so harsh, so petty and mean. My entire being wanted to scream out in agony and fright, yet could not. Carrying on day by day, dragging myself through life with an intent seriousness of Purpose. Yet not with joy, but with pain and deeply rooted sorrow.

Long have I known this was not the way, yet could not alter the pattern in order to let go of the burden of immense, crushing responsibility, knowing full well that responsibility must be joyful too. But I forgot how to play, so immersed was I in my mountain of duties.

The Angels listened patiently to my cries of pain. They saw the tears which would not flow. They felt the deep crevasse of my sorrow. Still they sang on and as they did, there was a stirring and a movement within my being. The energy which had long been blocked, began to move. I melted further into the haven of my pillows, letting go, releasing with one deep sigh the years of tears unshed.

And the winds of change did strongly blow, transmuting all that I let go. Sweeping away the old to make room for the new. Softly scouring my being until I surrendered fully. A sound of acceptance escaped my lips, echoing from star to star all the way into infinity.

Long lay I upon those silken pillows, sailing upon the Celestial oceans. Yet, it may have been only for an instant, for who marks time where none exists.

All I know is that I shall never, ever, be the

same. I have heard the stars sing out my name through Angelic song. Singing to the core of my Essence. What a balm to be understood and recognized, to be clearly seen and truly loved! The stars sing out to one of their own, welcoming me Home. They know that we are One. And in the miracle of being finally acknowledged as Myself, the painful manacles of separation are unlocked and fall away.

Now my tears flow freely, for I am back where I was ever meant to be. At Home amongst the stars. Each of us but a mirrored reflection of the One. Each of us adding our voice to the Song of All That Is.

My deepest yearnings wash away the dam of worldly illusion, take root and begin to flower. My ever opening heart expands to embrace the All as One. My starry brethren shed tears of joy as we merge back into what we truly are, One radiant Star of Love, floating upon the Celestial seas.

This is the peace of bliss. Nothing more and nothing less. The fullness of pure beingness.

The Planetary Grids

The Og-Min are controllers of the grid, maintaining and activating the various levels of the electromagnetic gridwork which encircles our planet.

The primary grid could be termed the *A Grid* or the *Master Grid*. It has been in position since the creation of this planet and contains few vortex points, most which are currently covered by oceans. The Master Grid is the underlying foundation grid setting the templates for planetary evolution.

The second grid is the one that most people are aware of and work with. This gridwork contains the planetary chakra systems. We can call it the *B Grid*. Emanating from this grid are the webbings of leylines which encircle the planet connecting major points or energy centers called vortexes along the grid. These leylines are pathways of energy conducting the planetary pulse to all the interconnected hub centers.

These vortex hubs come in various sizes and can be seen as domes, both great and small. The outward radiation from these vortexes vary, depending on whether or not they are activated. If they are, one will perceive a blossoming forth of energy from them, much like a fountain of Light.

Since the shifting of the etheric blueprint in 1988, many of the old B Grid vortexes have been undergoing profound restructurization and reassignment.

The full extent of this shift will become increasingly apparent with time. Ancient vortexes like Mt. Shasta and Glastonbury will be experiencing tremendous shifts in energy and focus. They are going through major reassignments of Purpose. Some places will begin a cycle of dormancy in order to undergo a thorough cleansing, well deserved rest and restructurization period. Others have just begun to be activated. It is like a changing of the guard done on a planetary vortex level. Important sceptres are being passed.

Likewise, new vortexes are ever being activated. Each of these places fulfills it own particular function that serves the whole. Some, like the multiple vortexes of Sedona, Arizona, are already becoming well known places of pilgrimage. Others shall only be perceived by a few. Each outward vortex or sacred place of power always has a corresponding hidden, inward vortex. Usually these are located near the outward focus, but in some instances, they can be quite distant geographically.

Whenever possible, I prefer to work with the hidden vortexes for they contain a quiet purity and depth of focus that is lacking in the more dramatically outward power centers. Many popular vortexes are inundated with an overload of unrefined psychic energy which makes subtle levels of interchange extremely difficult. Whenever I visit them, I spend much of my time either cleansing the vortex or healing breaches in the vortex webbing caused by overuse of both unrefined and misqualified energy.

Remain ever mindful to the beautiful, sacred places that call you. Some of them, though noticed by only a few, may be very important hidden planetary vortexes meant to be revered, protected and kept secret. This may be part of your sacred duty to this sweet Earth.

Although the B Grid vortex points are currently in the process of shifting, there are a few places where there is a rare alignment between of A and B Grid vortexes creating a Master Grid Vortex.

These are always places of major planetary significance. An obvious one is located at the site of the Great Pyramids in Giza, Egypt. Another is located on the South Island of New Zealand. This Master Grid Vortex was activated in 1991. Others are in the process of activating, as established B Grid vortexes shut down and new B Grid vortexes are activated. A few shall assuredly make the great alignment with a Master Grid Vortex in the times to come. It will be most interesting to see where these new Master Vortexes are located.

The third or C Grid encircling the planet is a protective overlay placed into position in 1986 when interdimensional warfare in a parallel dimension caused a breach into the B Grid. It is structured in a double X formation.

Harmonic Convergence

During the famous Harmonic Convergence in 1987, I had assumed that I would be on Mt. Shasta since that was where I was living at the time. Instead, about a week beforehand, I was led to a remote mountain lake that had to be hiked into. Here I was told, was where I was to spend Harmonic Convergence. This was a surprise, but quite acceptable, since two of my dearest friends and I had planned to spend the Convergence together.

The night before the big event, each of us received different instructions. My friend Gary, who is a gifted visionary artist, was to climb to the summit of Mt. Shasta, while the other one, Grace an Angelic poet who is the author of *A Language of Light,* was to remain at the base of the mountain. I was feeling somewhat left out, but luckily three other dear people manifested to come with me to our remote lake. They were my daughter Nova, a beloved star sister, and an ancient Chinese warrior who spent most of Convergence battling demons inside his tent.

By the afternoon of the first day of Convergence, I was still perplexed as to why my two beloved friends and I had been separated for this important planetary activation. It felt as if we were closely linked and yet I still carried doubts that perhaps I had gone to the wrong place. I wanted to be on Mt. Shasta with everyone else. Now I couldn't even see the mountain from where I was. Finally the light of understanding dawned. Standing on the shore of the lake in the midst of a small forest full of trees whose trunks and limbs were twisted in wild spirals as if caught in a surge of concentrated energy, I realized that I had been sent to Shasta's secret, inner vortex!

A few weeks before, I had written and circulated a message about the Doorway at Convergence. This message says in part:

> There shall be the opening of a Doorway, a crack between the worlds never before experienced. This moment shall come unannounced at some point between August 16th and 17th, 1987. Those who are consciously aware shall recognize this moment as the opening of a major dimensional doorway wherein exists no time / no space. This moment shall mark the ending of the old cycle and the beginning of the new. It shall be a pause between the in-going and the out-going breath...

Now I realized that Grace, Gary and I were each holding open a corner of a triangular shaped doorway. One at the summit of the mountain, one at the base and one at the hidden, inner vortex. We were connected to each other by Golden Threads of Light. How perfect it was! Remarkably, a few days later Gary returned from his journey to the summit of Mt. Shasta with an unusual poem he had written which had been inspired by the Lords of Light. It stated simply and beautifully:

We gave three candles
for the golden candelabra
by the door.
And said not a word
but let the little ones
pass by and enjoy
their Light.
And so by doing this
one small deed enabled
them also a glimpse
within our divine passage.
It was a gift of Father /
Mother God that we found
this opening and a gift
above also the three lights
on the stand.

. . . Gary Applegate

The Golden Grid

Since the anchoring of the new etheric blueprint followed by the subsequent Realignment of the Stars, there is an entirely new activation of the planetary grid, moving it into a New Octave.

This is caused by the establishment of a new Golden Grid framework suspended above the known planetary grids. Once in position, this Golden Grid expands into a crystalline lattice of starry webbing which encircles the planet. If you look down through the Golden Grid to the B grid below, you will notice an interplay of Light between the two grids which is of great importance. This view from above gives you the most accurate representation of the multi-dimensional effects of the alignment of the two grids.

The patterns in between the expanded Golden Grid and the lower B grid form a conversion / inversion zone, called an *Antarion Conversion* which is a translation station for the stepping up / stepping down of light frequency pulsations. When these zones are activated, much like the attraction of two magnets, a field of heightened energy is created. The area between the layers could be termed a *frequency null zone*. Its borders are bouncy with surface tension, much like the surface of water.

The vortex points on both grids are not in direct vertical alignment. Rather, they are aligned in diagonal trajectories. This is necessary in order to safely diffuse and disperse the energies. If these points of concentrated energy were vertically aligned, the focused energy would be too powerful and searing. Hence the diagonal alignment in which energy can be phased down to Earth in metered pulses. This term of measurement is called *phasar thrusts.*

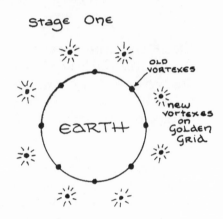

1. New Vortexes Form on Golden Grid

These pulsations of Light frequencies form triangles of Golden Light descending from the upper Golden Grid vortexes to vortexes on the Earth gridwork.

The sides of these triangles resemble multicolored chutes or tunnels of energy. If you draw a diagram of the Earth with the new Golden Grid points extending downwards to the planetary vortexes, you will discover that the planet now assumes the shape of a star!

As the triangles of Golden Light extend outwards from the planet, they also expand in an *inverted* manner creating tetrahedrons which extend the new star geometry into the planetary core thus forming the new starry skeleton for Earth's Light Body that she too, may transform into a star.

Once the new Golden Grid vortex points have been activated, a triangulation occurs, sending chutes of Light frequency pulsations Earthwards. As this energy exchange takes place between the vortexes on both old and new grids, there is a blossoming double helix of energy which activates the tetrahedrons. This blossoming proceeds until a full planetary transfiguration is achieved.

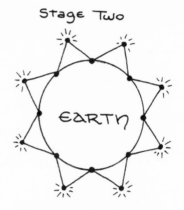

Stage Two

2. Activation of Golden Grid

The points located in between the old planetary vortexes now assume major significance forming new anchoring fields of Golden Light for the entire planet. This process intensely transforms the very nature of our planet, loosening the calcification of duality by placing more Light between the molecules. Thus Earth is developing her Light Body too!

Stage Three

Earth Becomes Star

3. Forming Starry Skeleton

A Gnome Initiation

Serving as the switchmen of the energy overlays in the conversion / inversion chutes of the frequency null zone are members of the gnome kingdom. Gnomes modulate the flow of currents, switching the frequencies from the new grid points to the old and back again. The only gnomes allowed to participate as grid switchmen are those who have undergone their starry initiation. I participated in one of these initiations in the forested farmlands of Quebec, and although I had not consciously worked with gnomes before, found it a most delightful experience.

I was visiting some friends in their farmhouse in the countryside of Quebec. One of them is a very respected geomancer and writer; someone with whom I have long shared my wilder visions. Both friends know that they are Angels and work closely with the planetary grid, activating domecaps around the planet. Recently, they have been communicating with gnomes who live at various sacred mountains as well as some in their garden at home.

Arriving at their house in early evening, we had a joyous visit. The following day around midday, I glanced outside into the garden at the rear of their house. To my great surprise, I noticed several gnomes walking about freely. They looked just like the pictures in *The Gnome Book*, only they were much taller than I expected, about two to three feet in height. I thought to myself that my friends must be quite well liked by the gnomes, to have them appear so openly.

A few hours later, I looked outside again and to my even greater surprise I saw that the rear garden was filled with hundreds of gnomes! A huge, festive pavilion had been erected at the back of the clearing and it appeared as if more gnomes were arriving each minute. I sensed that the woods surrounding the house were full of gnomes.

We immediately went outside to see what was going on. Well, it was a huge celebration complete with dancing gnomes doing funny little thumping dances to the music of kazoos, concertinas, drums & fiddles. There were gnomes setting out their wares to barter with each other like a marketplace and tents set up everywhere. In the back of the garden to the left of the pond was a row of shaggy, stout ponies, calmly grazing. More gnomes kept arriving from everywhere until there were thousands of gnomes. There were even gnomes from Lapland and some very cute Tyrolean gnomes wearing leiderhosen.

We were greeted by a most distinguished and slightly taller gnome named Dromedrill *pronounced Drom- Drom* who is the High King of this special gnome gathering. With utmost respect, he took us on a full tour, introducing us to many of the gnomes as if we were exalted guests of honor. One of these was Bromelor *pronounced Brom-Brom* who is the overseer of this part of Quebec. And feeling very Angelic *(my wings were quite expanded at the time)*, I was extremely aware of being an official representative of the Celestial Realms.

By late afternoon as we sat around the kitchen table, a hush descended upon our conversation, and we felt the Angels arriving. Waves upon waves of Angels were flying in, superimposed over each other in dimensional overlays. The skies filled with Angels as the most beautiful, peaceful energy of Love filled the room. The Heavenly Hosts had arrived! Now we knew for certain that something important was about to happen.

We sat quietly in the living room as dusk fell. My friend explained that long ago there was a pact between humans and gnomes. Humans agreed to take on the responsibility of periodically lifting the gnomes to the stars so that they could remember. But as humans forgot who they were, they also forgot many of their sacred duties. Hence gnomes were relegated to their chosen realms of the underworld without periodic reminders of their Divine origin.

But now in these accelerated times, much is changing. As humans remember that they are Angels, they are causing the spiral to turn. If the spiral turns for one of us, it turns for all, for we are truly One. So now is the time for the Angel-humans to fulfill their promise to the gnomes and bring them back into full remembrance by raising them to the stars. Except that this time it shall be done differently, for we are in the time of empowerment and mastery.

It was now dark outside, but this mattered not, for we had activated our full Sight. In the pond at the rear of the garden we saw a Golden Lotus rise out of the watery depths. Resting inside it was a large crystal egg. Golden Light spiraled in and out of the crystal egg. We now realized that we as Angels, are bringing the gift of the star to the gnomes. Inside the egg was a fragment of the Star That We Are.

Four of us who are awakened Angels stood on the Golden Lotus encircling the crystal egg. Between us stood four of the great Archangels—Mikael, Gabriel, Raphael & Uriel. Above the egg stood Metatron whose Presence was huge. The gnomes came up to us, four abreast in four columns, one from each of the four directions, to receive their star initiation. Each of us Angels touched the crystal egg with two fingers of our right hand as four small stars imbedded in our fingertips. In front of us was a row of four gnomes, waiting respectfully. They removed their red caps and bowed low before us. As they stood erect again, we touched them gently on the forehead, placing within them their very own star which shall help them remember and guide them home.

This represented a change in the ancient pact, for nevermore shall gnomes need to rely on humans for their glimpse of stars. Now they shall have their own. It is their time of graduation. As the Elohim planted stars within the humans long ago that one day we would remember, now the gnomes have been presented with their own stars by humans who have remembered that they are Angels. For both humans and gnomes, stars are the keys to our completion. How perfect it is!

I heard fragments of an ancient gnomesong, long remembered, but never fully understood. Encoded within it is the story of this very moment, prophesying this initiation in the cryptic language of the Mysteries. Singing of the day when Angels would return to Earth and give the gnomes the greatest of gifts, their starry maps home. Tonight this song encircled the planet, sung by gnomes everywhere, yet sung in a fuller version that revealed its hidden depth.

As the gnomes received their stars, a profound change within them was seen. They appeared to get younger before our very eyes, weariness dropped away, wrinkles lightened, their skin smoothed out, and most wondrously, their eyes emanate a starry twinkle! Even their beards have disappeared. Yet I know that the gnomes shall appear unchanged to all except those who also carry the star. From this night forward, the nature of gnomeservice on Earth shall be vastly different. They have moved to a higher octave. The fulfillment of the ancient pact has moved the Golden Spiral to another level. As subterranean star carriers the gnomes shall transport the stars underground to places where humans could never take them. This in turn, will help transform Earth into a star.

Still the gnomes filed forward in a never-ending procession. We continuously dispensed stars to the gnomes as everything—garden, pond, lotus, crystal egg, lines of gnomes, Angels, Archangels—fused into a column of brilliant Golden White Light. Above our Pillar of Light shines the radiant One Star.

Finally, only one gnome awaited initiation. It was Dromedrill the High King. Already, the crystal egg had begun to dissolve. I reached inside it and touched the fragment of star inside it. With this star, Dromedrill was initiated and thus shall he now be able to initiate other gnomes. As the crystal egg fully dissolved, the lotus descended to the bottom of the pond. Metatron called the four of us forth and placed a gnomestar within our foreheads. Thus shall gnomes and fairies everywhere recognize us as starfriends. A gnomeshrine called a gnomecile, was later created at the rear of the pond, serving as a place of pilgrimage for gnomes everywhere.

Altogether, quite a remarkable adventure! The following morning before we left, I glanced out to the back yard. All of the gnomes appeared to be gone, but there was still an etheric residue of the momentous events of the previous evening. Although everything looked the same on the physical level, you could still feel the crushed grass where the ponies had nibbled and tramped and hear the joyful strains of gnomemusic wafting on the memories of the wind. And as we drove away for miles and miles, I swear I saw a line of gnomes proudly wearing gleaming stars upon their foreheads, bowing to us, red caps in hand.

Antarion Conversion

The Antarion Conversion represents the method in which heightened energies are relayed to Earth from multi-dimensional frequencies.

It was placed into activation in 1987, heralding the entrance of a new energy patterning. This energy pattern has unusual dimensional forcefield co-sine frequencies, creating an inversion system which now allows Earth to act as a receptor unit.

The inversion system known as the Antarion Conversion is located in the intersection of the X in the first diagram. It is also known as the 12:21. This is to signify that whatever passes through that intersection shall be

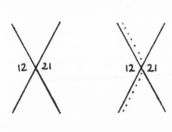

reversed, not merely in direction, but in a manner which could be perceived as *inside out.* This conversion is in effect regardless of which direction the energy passes through, whether it is *coming* or *going,* so to speak.

A thorough reversal of the heightened frequency transmission is necessary in order for it be received, understood and assimilated by those on Earth. Until 1987, the reception of these energy frequencies was not possible, since our cellular restructurization had yet to reach a certain level of multi-dimensional awareness.

A simpler form of Antarion Conversion was once used upon this planet long ago when the energy emanation of AN was in physical existence. This was during the time period from early Lemuria until the first sinking of Atlantis. After that, the AN manifestation was withdrawn from physical expression in its pure form, although those of the AN lineage have continued to serve here, founding the Egyptian and Inca civilizations among others. In the chapter of my book, *The Legend of Altazar* titled *The Tower of Light,* you will find an experience of the Antarion Conversion as practiced in those faraway times.

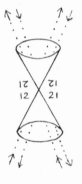

The Antarion Conversion shall be perceived as a transmitter / receiver battery or as a stepping up / stepping down station.

When energy patterns enter the inversion system they reverse like a mirror image of themselves, then proceed in a diagonal patterning of vibratory pulsations. This alters and lightens the intensity of the pulsation frequency which otherwise could not enter dimensions three and four.

This inversion system also functions as a *translation station* altering encoded pulsations of light frequencies into genetic patternings which can be more easily understood and assimilated by us. The translation station serves to reposition encoded light frequencies into measured units of energy containing precise pattern sequencing and timing cycles called *phasar thrusts.*

Phasar thrusts regulate the speed, direction and intensity of the incoming and outgoing energy pulsations. They somewhat resemble Morse Code in their patternings of dots and dashes. Phasar thrusts always enter and depart through a diagonal trajectory. Once again, this energy is too powerful to manifest in a direct vertical alignment.

Energy always enters and departs the Antarion Conversion system in a spiral patterning. If you lightly trace a spiral in the air, you will see that it moves on a constant diagonal path, steadily rotating direction, like a series of switch-back roads. It never moves in a horizontal or vertical patterning.

The energy transference within the center of the X located in the middle of the Antarion Conversion overlaps as it reverses itself. *(What I referred to as turning itself inside out.)* This causes the two cones of influence to interlock, thus creating an opening or doorway which was previously imperceptible.

These cones represent any two polarities such as spirit and matter, past and future, or good and evil. They also delineate the boundaries of our probable realities. Thus the applications of the Antarion Conversion are manifold. The importance of this multi-dimensional doorway lies in its potential to merge and ultimately, to transcend, two opposite spheres of influence.

Not only is the Antarion Conversion in effect above this planet upon the higher dimensional spheres, but when we develop a state of conscious multi-dimensionality, the Antarion Conversion can be accessed within our own beings.

Once recognized, it can be utilized by us on both personal and planetary levels. Ultimately, we ourselves become Antarion Conversions, serving as dimensional doorways and zones of merger and overlap between varied vibrational patternings.

The doorway in the center of the Zone of Overlap within the Antarion Conversion could also be perceived as the *Zone of Oneness*. Here is the doorway which leads to the Unknown. And this is the entry point to the 11:11. Once activated within your being, you are granted full access to explore in myriad directions. You are directly connected to unlimited storehouses of knowledge. It is not necessary to hold this knowledge in your conscious memory, for that would truly be overwhelming. Rather, knowing that you have full access to the Unknown, you are free to enter the field of the Antarian Conversion and retrieve whatever you need whenever it is required.

Space Beings

Although most people lump together *space beings, star beings* **and** *Angels* **under the label of extraterrestrials, there is a vast difference in energy between them.**

Space beings emanate from numerous levels of awareness, but are still subject to the limitations of duality. A great deal of finely honed discernment is necessary when you are dealing with *space* energies. Not all extraterrestrial contacts are here for your Highest Good. Some of them are subtly insinuating their presence on this planet for rather ignoble causes. I cannot stress strongly enough the need to use utmost discernment when dealing with space energies.

Today there is a great deal of fascination with space entities. Many people are contacting various space brotherhoods without having full knowledge of what this entails. Much of the distorted space energies are coming from the fourth dimensional astral sphere where illusion runs rampant. It is important to remember that not all space beings are highly evolved. Many of them, although more technologically advanced than us, are severely lacking in the development of their emotional bodies. There is a cold detachment about them, for they do not understand the emotion of Love. One of the main reasons that they are being drawn to the Earth in such large numbers is so they can learn about Love. Actually, we have a great deal to teach them!

As to the phenomena of *walk-ins* which is currently popular, it is important to see this with greater clarity. Before we offer to give up our bodies and souls so readily, perhaps we should consider just where our souls are going to go and how we are going to retrieve them later. Because eventually, they shall have to be retrieved. Whatever we are trying to avoid dealing with by vacating our bodies, will have to be faced and resolved, sooner or later. Walking-out is somewhat like committing suicide; it may temporarily relieve the symptoms, but it is definitely not going to solve the problem. Remember, *the only way out is in!*

If you really want to be complete on the earthplane, then you must bring your full Presence into the physical to gain your freedom. No half measures are going to do it.

It greatly saddens me to find people willingly setting aside their bodies and souls to alien entities. Not all alien entities currently embodying are here to serve humanity. Do you really want to become an android? In some cases that I have encountered, this is precisely what is happening. You can read the signs when a person's inner circuitry is tampered with. This manifests as an impersonal cold mentalness along with severe emotional imbalances. There is a crude splicing and rewiring within the central nervous system. What this does is short circuit the individual's own direct connection to the One. Whenever their own spiritual energies reach a certain heightened level of awareness, the sabotage mode activates a shut down of their higher consciousness.

I've seen a lot of strange things in my journey through life. I don't like to dwell on these energies, but they are present on certain dimensional levels and sometimes have to be dealt with. If you want to know what octave a being is coming from, simply sense their energy with your heart. Do you feel an abundance of love or do you sense a superior arrogance and coldness? Please, listen to your heart!

Space beings also differ from starry beings in that they often travel in space ships.

These ships vary greatly in dimensional octave from the lower frequency astral ships which are metallic in composition to those which are concentrations of light pulses. Space beings have myriad forms, some of which are quite strange or frightening to perceive, although these are often initially disguised under a weak veneer of humanness. It helps to develop your ability to see beyond the outer form.

A few years ago there was a breach in Earth's protective grid overlay enabling some unsavory space entities to enter. This was in violation of sacred agreements made under the jurisdiction of the Interplanetary Commission protecting Earth from unwanted influences. Aliens are walking among us in numbers far vaster than anyone suspects. Just what their purpose is here, we can only guess. However, we would urge you to be cautious with space aliens and with people who channel space entities. There is a dangerous manipulation from beings who sneak onto this planet, do cattle mutilations, make implants and other human experiments and take over innocent, though unresisting souls. I realize that this sounds like the wildest science fiction, but it is happening among us today and deserves greater awareness.

The space alien vibration is entirely different than the Angelic frequency which is rooted in Love. When your Angel comes in and anchors within you, *your own* Higher Self unites with you. You don't become taken over by someone else, but become more yourself than ever before.

There are also some highly evolved space beings who are observing our planet in order to aid us in our transition to the Greater Reality.

They are members of the Inter-Galactic Star Confederation who originate from the major star systems and stargates which we visit between our earthly incarnations. These are the Star Commanders of the starfleets. Strongly upholding Divine Law with unwavering obedience, they exhibit a deep sense of loving compassion and dedicated service to *all* humanity, not just the chosen few.

They have two main headquarters bases on this planet, one in the Gobi Desert in Mongolia, the other in a remote location in the western United States. These bases are not hidden to those who can See and have the impeccable integrity not to misuse what they See. The base in the United States emits a most beautiful music of celestial choirs when one comes into its sphere. The gateway to it is well marked, but not visible to normal, human vision.

The primary concern of the Star Confederation is that we might destroy this planet, as has happened many times before. Especially since Earth has willingly given refuge to many survivors from Mars, Maldek and other planets who have destroyed themselves. They are still learning intense lessons on the abuse of power.

Maldek is the planet previously located between Mars and Jupiter which blew itself up and became the Asteroid Belt. There are enclaves of Maldekians in clustered spots upon this planet. Although they promised to refrain from their previous activities misusing power, some of them are surreptitiously at it again, being particularly drawn to all facets of the nuclear energy industry, from manufacturing to public relations. There are cities and towns in the United States which have large concentrations of this type of aliens living in them, particularly in eastern Utah & eastern Idaho.

The Star Confederation also closely observes activities which emanate from portions of Orion including its subsidiary of Draco. Even parts of the Pleiadian High Command have been infiltrated by the dark lords of Orion. Thus some of that which is presented to us from the Pleiades is not of true Pleiadian purity. Not all energies originating from Orion are negative in nature. The area of the belt called the EL*AN*RA which we shall discuss later, is one of the key energy outposts of this dimensional universe. And there is also the star Betelguese which is home to the Councils of Light. However, some misguided Orion energy from the area of Rigel seeded much misuse of power during the times of Atlantis. That is why we are still dealing with these issues today.

These matters have been brought to your attention simply so you can be aware that they do exist, especially in the fourth dimensional astral plane which most of us are still susceptible to in our present level of consciousness. As we have stated before, we are not here to lend our energies to any battle between dark and light. What is perceived as *the dark* is merely one half of duality. We are here to bring healing and wholeness both to ourselves and to the entire planet. We achieve this by embodying Oneness.

Our task is to be such impeccable Pillars of Light that our Unified Presence releases and magnifies the flow of the immense Love of Oneness that it may go forth freely to all.

This planet is as much of a melting pot as the United States ever was. Beings are here from all over the galaxy, as well as many dimensional universes. Earth has not taken upon herself just the laggards and malcontents from other civilizations. In the initial colonization periods of this planet, some of the finest, brightest beings, including many of royal lineages from other star systems were sent here in order to aid in this grand adventure of transcending duality. Many of them still serve among us today. They too, are in the process of fulfilling their Higher Purpose.

The Intergalactic Confederation

8.8.88

The Intergalactic Confederation hereby proclaims the establishment of an energy modulation arc calibrated to a psi frequency overlay. This arc connects the two Headquarters bases on planet Earth in order to stabilize planetary rotation through an emanation of co-sine frequencies.

This will make it possible for Earth to receive fifth dimensional octaves in ever increasing magnificance. You shall notice the effect of this almost immediately. That is why you are experiencing the sensation of expectancy, awaiting the impending arrival of something of vast importance.

Indeed, the very grid and leylines of this planet are being greatly affected at this very moment as the arc is locked into position. Had this not happened, the Earth would have experienced massive physical shifts during this period. A state of Divine Intervention is in effect.

With the placement of the arc came the arrival of

the Heavenly Hosts. Many of the Great Ones have turned their attention to this small planet in order to facilitate and witness its birth into the fifth dimensional frequency emanation. As you turn your attention to them, you will feel their Divine Presence within you. Indeed, your Starry Overself is working in close partnership with them. You are acting as both a transmitter and a receiver of fifth directional stabilization frequencies.

This arc is of a Golden hue with many shimmering, shifting rainbow Lights upon it, especially magenta, yellow, aqua and rose—clear, translucent colors. As you place the arc within your inner sight, you can hear its sound as it sweeps across the atmosphere of Earth. Ah --aa--aa--aa--a, fluctuating rapidly. This sound serves to deionize matter, softening the calcification of its particles, which shall allow it to transmute duality more gently as it dissolves its rigidity.

The barriers of separation between individualized units of matter are melting away. This effect shall continue to be enhanced with the passing of time allowing an increased sense of Oneness as the illusion of separation steadily disappears. Truly the time is at hand whereby we begin to merge into the vast, overriding state of Oneness.

You may see yourselves as anchors of the stars. For through the Golden tubes of your being, the Earth shall be permeated with Golden Stars, tiny fragments of the Great, Golden White Star.

Planetary Wobble

Currently, there is a state of instability along the internal axis of this planet creating a Planetary Wobble.

If we go within the Earth using our inner sight, we will see a hollow chute which connects the two magnetic poles. Inside this chute runs a thin Golden Thread which protrudes out of both ends of the planet. This is the Golden Beam which keeps our planet in rotational position as well as maintaining the correct alignment and balance for our entire solar system within its galaxy.

Normally, the Golden Beam fills the entire hollow chute or tubing which runs between Earth's magnetic poles. However, for some reason which I am not given to see, either the beam has narrowed or the chute has enlarged. What this has created is a most unstable wobble within this planet.

A year ago when I first discovered this condition, I made an interesting journey to the central core of Earth. Usually I go there directly, from sitting in my room to being there instantly, without any traveling in between. In the center of the Earth is a Golden Sun surrounded by crystal beds. We have done much work there activating the crystals by placing within them tiny Golden Stars from our One Golden, White Star. You might say that we have been Star Aligning the planet.

Well, my strange journey to the center of the Earth began innocently enough. I was sitting quietly when I was called inwards. I soon discovered myself traveling through space in a little space vehicle, somewhat shaped like a bullet car which held me and another passenger behind me. I was driving this thing like I knew what I was doing!

At first, I assumed that we were going to travel somewhere mysterious and faraway in space, but that was not to be the case. We arced high up in the sky and zoomed into an opening near the North Pole before I even had time to catch my breath.

Now began the really exciting part as we raced through the labyrinthine tunnels inside the planet. And I mean raced! I drove that little vehicle so fast, that we were a blur of Light, shifting the controls so rapidly in order to maneuver through the twists and turns of the labyrinth, that I couldn't see my hands move. Somehow, amazingly, I seemed to know exactly what I was doing and where we were going. I felt as if I had a map imprinted within my molecules and had done this many times before.

And it is true that there are worlds within this world. I saw mountains and valleys, settlements of people, beautiful skies and a profusion of different types of scenery as we zoomed by. (Luckily, even scientists have recently discovered the existence of mountain ranges

*inside the Earth. I read about it in Time Magazine.) The
entire trip was fascinating, but quick. Before I knew it,
we had arrived at the center of the Earth. There I
discovered this immense wobble. Even the central core
was resounding with banging and crashing sounds.*

*Then and there, I began to call in more Golden
Light, magnifying the intensity of the Golden Beam so
that it would fill up the empty space in the tubing. This
greatly alleviated the instability between the two axis
points. But I feel that it was only a temporary measure
and that to truly heal this situation calls for a more
concerted effort.*

*Therefore, I Call out to all of you to join with me in
raising the vibrational intensity of the Golden Beam
which passes through this planet. Let us join together in
our Unified Presence and call forth to our Star, the Star
That We Are, to send its radiance to strengthen the
Golden Beam. I feel that this is of critical importance at
this time and I hope that some of you do too. Actions
such as this are part of our collective and individual
responsibilities as instruments of Divine Intervention.*

While presently unstable, the Planetary Wobble is
serving to shift our present state of conscious
awareness. It is preparing to move this planet, as well
as this dimensional universe, into a New Octave. By the
year 2011 as we make our collective ascension, the
wobble will shift us into alignment with a new Pole
Star, which is currently outside the line of vision of our
past and future probable realities. This Pole Star is
already in position, quite near to us actually, awaiting
our alignment into its sphere of influence.

Stargates

It could be said that there are many doors in and one door out.

We are referring here to this dimensional universe which contains dimensions one through six. As we arrived here from what we shall term, *Beyond the Beyond,* we chose an individual entry point or *midway station* which indicated our preferred mode of expression. These stargates could be perceived as separate notes upon a unified scale or as fingers upon the same hand. Many of them are familiar to us as Sirius, Arcturus, Orion, Antares, Pleiades, Andromeda, Aldebaron, Polaris, etc. Some of us have felt as if these stargates were our homes. Although we have long immersed ourselves in their vibratory frequencies, finding great solace in their familiarity, often returning to them between earthly embodiments, they are not our places of origin. They simply represent our gateway to the Beyond.

As we travel from this dimensional universe to the next, we journey through these stargates which can be perceived as *black holes*. During the process of passing through a black hole, like an eye of a needle, we proceed down a long, winding black tunnel at a rapid pace. This tunnel is actually a spiral which leads us into the center of the black hole. Please note the similarity with the death process. This is not coincidental; it is merely a kindred experience of shifting dimensions.

I might mention that the reason why astronomers believe that no light ever escapes a black hole, is because it travels to another dimension where it is not perceptible from this one.

As we move through the entry way of the black hole, there is a great shucking off and dissolving away of all elements of our beings incapable of passing through the eye of the needle.

It's as if all the garments you have worn throughout an entire incarnation or cycle of embodiments are rapidly stripped away until only purest Essence remains. Essence is the only part of what was perceived of as *you* which can pass through the black hole into the higher dimensional frequency.

When you approach this same opening from the other side of the Beyond, it is experienced quite differently. From here it is perceived as a *white hole,* which means that there is a funnel shaped vortex which shapes unlimited Essence into a fine pinpoint of Light which then passes through the eye of the needle. Once through the center of the white hole, the cloaks of individuality are donned. Soon you find yourself at the destination of your preordained stargate.

So many times have we made the journey back and forth through the dimensional doorways of stargates, that we even do it when we are asleep. It has become something that many of us do with great ease, whether consciously or unconsciously. We have developed full rights of passage through our chosen stargate into the Beyond and back.

Some of us have expanded our consciousness sufficiently to enable us to travel through more than one major stargate, obtaining a comfortable sense of being home in several stargates. We have developed the ability to tune into different frequencies of energy and express them whenever we choose. This familiarity with more than one major stargate helps free us from a primary identification with just one stargate. It enables us to stretch our awareness to the outer boundaries of this dimensional universe. As our consciousness ever expands, we start to realize that our true being is too vast to be contained solely within dimensions one through six.

Thus we begin to hear the Call of the Unknown. This is where many of us Star-Borne ones are today. We have expanded our parameters beyond Earth, beyond this solar system, beyond this galaxy, beyond this dimension, ever beyond. We are opening ourselves up by becoming ever vaster, singing the *Song of One* which leads us Home.

• We do not return Home through the doorways which brought us here.

• And we do not return Home as separate units of consciousness.

• We do not get evacuated by space ships, nor do we go anywhere with stress and suffering.

• We ourselves, create our homeward vehicle, and we do this by merging together in love and reuniting into the One.

• The One is our homeward vehicle. It is our crystalline star, *the Star that We Are!*

Before we can merge together with others of our Starry Family, we must first unite with our Higher Selves, our Golden Solar Angel. This is our vast Starry Overself. For only then are we capable of joining with others in our Unified Presence. We come together in the full Light of conscious remembrance as the Golden Rays of One Star. And now we must prepare ourselves in order to create the homeward vehicle.

Each star is an energy station . . .

Like snowflakes, no two are alike . . .

Every star has its own mandala . . .

Each of us corresponds to the mandala
of our own star . . .

Within our DNA is encoded the pattern
of our star . . .

Each of us is an outpost of the energy station
of our star . . .

We are diluted projections of our star . . .

All of our stars are fragments of One Star . . .

United together, our starry fragments form

The Great Central Sun

Of the One.

Planetary Transference

We did not descend directly to Earth from our chosen stargate or midway station.

Instead, another stage of the stepping down of energies was necessary in order to enter this planet's gravitational field. This is what we refer to as planetary transference. The planets within Earth's own solar system have long served as transfer points. You can perceive them as schools or temples of varied emanations, each one perfectly suited to attune the cosmic traveler to the needed aspects of awareness.

Some of you might remember serving in the Temples of Venus or in the great Councils of Saturn. There are also the Halls of Creativity on Uranus and the deep Mystery Schools of Pluto. Each planet in our solar system has long functioned as a school of initiation for mastery upon the earthplane. With the exception of Maldek which destroyed itself, and Mars who suffered a similar fate, in a very different manner.

Δ

Tiny Mercury is the center of intellect, fostering the fullest development of the Higher Mind. Possibly in previous incarnations if you didn't develop your mental powers, you might spend time on Mercury before entering Earth for an embodiment which stressed intellectual growth.

Δ

Venus is well known for its Seven Temples which are under the rulership and guidance of the great Sanat Kumara and the royal family of Kumaras. In times past there were always seven Kumaras in physical embodiment upon Earth. Now however, in these accelerated times, that number has jumped to seventy seven.

Each of the Seven Holy Temples of Venus, beautiful white domed buildings, has seeded a Kumara. Now each Kumara has embodied into eleven beings who walk among you on Earth. These seventy seven of the direct lineage of our holy father, Sanat Kumara, are here to serve mankind by awakening, empowering & initiating those who choose to answer the Call, and most importantly, by embodying the Essence of their sacred Venusian Temples.

Venus was the final entry point for the seventy seven blessed ones, though their true origin lies Beyond the Beyond. Their journey has been vast to come to Earth. Often do they return to their beloved Venus in order to receive further instructions and immersion into pure Essence, although part of them eternally resides within the hallowed Temples of Venus.

Now these seventy seven do prepare to complete their earthly span of service to once again travel beyond the gateways where they may serve ever more fully upon the Starry Councils overseeing the evolution of entire galactic systems.

In their final years on Earth, the Kumaras are here to activate the Golden Solar Angels of the Great Central Sun, for it is time for them to fly as One.

The Seven Holy Temples of Venus are:

1. *Temple of Empowerment – from whence comes*
   Service & Duration.

2. *Temple of Purity – from whence comes*
   Grace & Innocence.

3. *Temple of Divine Love – from whence comes*
   Beauty & Devotion.

4. *Temple of Compassion – from whence comes*
   Healing & Nourishment.

5. *Temple of Truth – from whence comes*
   Clarity & Vision.

6. *Temple of Divine Law – from whence comes*
   Justice & Integrity.

7. *Temple of Wisdom – from whence comes*
   Knowledge & Enlightenment.

Together they create the Temple of Ascension, which
is the capstone of all Seven Holy Temples combined
– from whence comes Freedom & Oneness.

Δ

Mars served as a center of power, training those who
came to Earth to serve in leadership capacities. Alas
long ago, there was a terrible war on Mars and the two
mighty civilizations which had flourished there in
harmony until near the end destroyed each other, so
nothing remains except the ruins of magnificent
pyramids and temples. Possibly this is why power
remains such an issue during these present times and
why it is so rare to find individuals who can be clean,
Divinely inspired instruments of power.

Mars definitely had a strong role to play in the long history of fair Atlantis, which began so beautifully and had such an ignoble end. During the latter days of the Atlantean civilization, life degenerated into open arrogance, manipulation and control, culminating in its tragic demise. The same old story that had initially taken place on Mars, played itself out again without reaching final resolution. Even today, it continues.

Unfortunately, the Temples of Mars are no longer in operation and we must learn our lessons of power and the wise use of energy from other sources. This has resulted in rather haphazard schooling in these matters for most of Earth's current inhabitants as well as a constant cycle of wars.

Warriors belong to the sphere of Mars and were the Martian Temples still intact, they would be learning even now that the highest octave of warriorship is to rise into kingship. For that is what warriors evolve into after they have mastered the proper balance of energy and power with responsibility and compassion.

Δ

Inside the hallowed Halls of Jupiter is learned the art of expansion, as well as the inherent Oneness of all. The teachings given here are of joy and abundance, thus it is a most popular and requested transference zone. Perhaps, that's why this planet is so large, in order to handle all the crowds. When one has carried the burdens of responsibility for too long and suffered great hardships in previous embodiments, then one is often sent to the Halls of Jupiter to rediscover laughter and lightness of being.

Δ

Of course, if you've spent a lot of time on Jupiter, it's probably time for you to visit Saturn. Within the massive Councils of Saturn the evolutionary template of this solar system is implemented. Beings from the entire galaxy frequently visit Saturn in order to confer about these weighty matters. This is the planet of responsibility and concentrated focus. On Saturn you feel the weight of the balance of wisdom and responsibility resting heavily upon your shoulders. Correct procedure is carefully pondered and sought after. You learn about the wise use of authority and its inherent burdens. Often after several indulgent lifetimes, you will be assigned to a tour of duty on Saturn. This usually straightens you out fast!

Δ

Uranus is the center of Creativity. The energy intensely vibrates with electrical currents. In the Temples of Creativity on Uranus, you learn about Divine Inspiration, often in a most unsettling manner. Uranus is the home of the unexpected, that sudden burst of creative inspiration that comes from out of nowhere like a bolt of lightning. It's not known for being restful here; but it is definitely exciting! Uranus contains a direct open channel to Beyond the Beyond, so here you will experience new energies which are not directly available within the rest of the solar system. Many messengers from the higher realms who are serving on Earth receive direct transmissions through a Uranian transference. This is why they are capable of bringing in the new and unknown.

Δ

Neptune is soft and dreamy. Its Temples are dedicated to the Visionary and the Mystic. Everything here is moist, even the air has a gentle mist to it. There is little physical activity on Neptune, instead you could observe most of the inhabitants sleeping peacefully. For this is the languid land of the Dreamer. Within their dreams are both mystical revelations and illusions. Their lesson is to experience the worlds of dreams and visions and eventually to learn how to discern what is real and what is illusion. After serving in the Temples of Neptune, you descend to Earth in order to serve as priests and mystics, sages and dreamers, wanderers and saints.

Δ

Pluto is the most intense of the planetary centers of learning. Within its magnetic Mystery School you face the core issues of life and death itself, undergoing a steady cycle of deep initiations into hidden wisdom. It is the planet of Transformation, of death and renewal, the home of the legendary Phoenix. Pluto is not an easy place to visit and far fewer come here than to the other planets. Not being a place for beginners, it is saved for advanced initiates, ones who have proved themselves strong and enduring through repeated testing. This is the planet of the final Initiation into the Unknown and is definitely not a place for the faint hearted, as its teachings are profoundly powerful and deep.

Δ

Possibly now that you are more familiar with the centers of planetary transference, you can identify the ones where you have been taught and prepared for your earthly embodiments. Many people have yet to undergo initiations in various planetary temples. Yet, to regain wholeness through the full spectrum of experience, we must eventually experience initiation in each holy temple.

To keep this all in perspective, I would like to add that it is merely the tiny fragment of our vast Angelic Self who has visited these planets at all, for that is the only portion of our being who experiences incarnations upon this planet.

Sanat Kumara:

Beloved Ones of the Great Central Sun, we honor you for your dedicated service to humanity. We have now entered the Time of Completion soon to be followed by the radiant Golden Dawn. We have all long awaited this moment.

The sacred spiral doth turn. You yourselves, have aided in this process by your reawakening, both as individuals and as a collective whole. As the spiral turns, much shall be left behind. This is as it should be, for you must be unencumbered by the weight of your past in order to face the future freely.

Beloved sons & daughters of the stars, your long journey to remember is almost over. Nevermore shall you experience forgetfulness of your Divine Origin & Heritage, for the lengthy process of the transmutation of duality has nearly been achieved.

We stand on the brink of a New Octave wherein we must be fully conscious, empowered beings. This New Octave signals the entrance into higher realms of awareness termed Supra-Normal.

Ever do I watch over you with deepest love. My
Kumaras walk among you to help bring you Home.
Together we are going to reanchor the energies of
Shamballa upon this planet. However, this time it shall
not be found upon just one physical location, but it will
be within the hearts of all who have awakened to the
Greater Reality. For Shamballa is the manifestation of
the Greater Reality. It shall be birthed once again upon
Earth as was promised by me long ago when I removed
its energies from its previous anchorage in the Gobi
Desert in Mongolia.

This time, the radiance of Shamballa will
illuminate the entire planet from within the hearts of
awakened humanity. Thus shall you experience a direct
infusion of the Greater Reality allowing you to achieve
freedom and mastery from the time / space continuum.
And experience a greater ease and fluidity of being than
ever before.

The choice is up to you. The Kumaras are among
you right now calling you Home, serving as the anchors
of Shamballa and messengers of the Golden Dawn.

An / On

The uniting of two opposite polarities into Oneness is the energy known as AN or ON.

AN represents the union of Sun and Moon into One Being. (AN is also mentioned in my earlier book, *The Legend of Altazar.*) The information given is for the purpose of triggering your own cellular memories of AN if you are connected with this star lineage.

In earlier times AN was an important influence on this planet, then the Kingdom of AN disappeared from history as the Earth was immersed in the experience of duality. Now that we are entering the Time of Completion and preparing for our ascension into a new Template of Oneness, the energy focus of AN is once again making itself felt. Those individuals aligned with AN are currently being reactivated that they may take their appropriate positions within the spiral of the Invisible.

Though both AN and ON are pronounced *on*, the difference in their spellings represent two diverse manifestations of the Essence of AN. The AN is a rising up while ON is an opening out. If you belong to either of the two twin emanations of AN, you will recognize it within your own heart. It will resonate within your cells and perhaps even move you to tears.

Teton Initiation

In 1988 during the Blue Moon in May, I was called to the Teton Mountains in Wyoming. Though I had heard much about the secret Councils in the Tetons, I had never before visited there in the physical. I had no idea what I might encounter, but knew that I must make the journey. It was with great excitement that with a friend, I set off for quite an adventure!

A few nights before we departed I received the following message:

Both of you are ready,
the years of preparation passed.
You remember now;
you have awakened.
You are embodying
that which you truly are.
Now is the time
to sit in your appointed positions
as living representatives of the Council
serving in human forms.

There shall be four steps.
Monday night will be the foundation.

Tuesday, you will enter the portals,
bypassing the labyrinth,
stepping up through dimensional octaves,
much like a switch-back system of roads,
rising upwards in a lightning pattern.

Entering the Chamber
by appointed invitation,
the Council shall await
with great joy at your arrival.
Around you are vast treasures,
yet, details matter not
for you shall don your robes
and receive a starry gift.
as the Heavens open wide.

Wednesday shall be Sacred Union
of Heaven and Earth.
Instructions will be received
as pre-encoded memories are activated
in unceasing transmissions.
entering the Zone of Silence
wherein all things can be heard.
Thus shall you be further prepared
for your full emergence & activation
into Octave Seven leading to Octave Eleven.
The El*An*Ra shall be imprinted.
The Crystal Mountain calls its own.
4 · 7 · 11: Journey to 22.
The combined 22s birth the 44.
AN is here.
The apex of AN rises
above the mists of time
for all to see.
A Starry Beacon.
Encoded pulsations of Light

flashing through layers of density,
penetrating the veils,
preparing the gathering together
which leads to Return.

This Beacon, this Eye of AN,
once established and anchored,
shall see and be seen,
shall know and be known.
It is the point of connection
between 4 & 44.
Eleven is the Door.
You are the key.

*The first evening in the Tetons passed peacefully.
There was a light rain and the mountains were covered
in misty fog, adding to the atmosphere of impending
mystery. The fatherly Presence of Sanat Kumara felt
extremely close, wrapping me in a powerful aura of love.
As I tuned into the Councils, I could feel them bustling
with preparations for our arrival. I felt very humble, like
a little girl who was about to meet her family. Before we
went to sleep, I received a short message from Sanat
Kumara:*

I Am Sanat Kumara.
The Voice of the Central Sun.

My daughters, we welcome you to our Teton
Retreat. Long have we awaited this moment. It is with
loving anticipation that our Council Chambers have
been prepared to receive you.

This experience could be likened unto your
graduation, for indeed, you have completed an entire
phase of experience that has spanned the total cycle of
your earthly embodiments. This impending initiation

symbolizes the moment wherein you may now shed your skins, so to speak, and be raised into a new frequency grid patterning.

Much awaits you within this new grid matrix. Tomorrow you will receive encoded information which will serve you to make a quantum leap adjustment.

Tonight the emphasis is on the shedding of the outer garments / skins, integrating what is yet unresolved, & your formal entry and installation into the Council.

We spent the next day hiking through the drizzle, exploring the Tetons. They felt increasingly familiar to me, so beautifully majestic and noble. I ate copious amounts of food, as I had been doing for the past two days. Somehow, four or five meals a day were almost enough. It wasn't that I was hungry, but I simply needed to eat until I was uncomfortably stuffed. This served me as ballast. It certainly felt like I had a lead weight inside my stomach, keeping me thoroughly pinned to Earth. Throughout the day, I was constantly being pulled away to other dimensions and was most grateful that I did not have to drive.

That evening we sat in the back of our minivan parked in the campground. A light rain was still falling, just enough to stay inside. I was fortunate to be on this journey with an ancient star sister who has a vast capability for seeing. It was the first time that we had worked together in this manner. We decided that we were ready to experience whatever awaited us. Becoming quiet, we tuned into the energies which gently swirled around us. This is what we experienced:

We began with a phase of integration and completion. I merged with Solaris Antari, the male aspect of my Angel. He and Solara became one. My friend united with a magenta and gold beam.

Together we were taken to the third level of a step pyramid. Side by side, we walked up the stairs carrying a star lantern between us. The moon was magenta rimmed in gold, which signified that AN was present.

I watched the four directions transform themselves into eleven directions in the form of a crystalline star edged in gold. Then we went up a large white stairway towards a massive round wooden door at the top of the stairs. The door had a heavy metal ring hanging from it.

As the door opened, many Light Beings descended both sides of the stairway to welcome us. They wore ceremonial white brocaded robes edged in gold. Upon their heads were tall, white and gold hats, shaped like the hats of Tibetan Lamas. In the center of these hats were small discs of AN which glowed magenta and golden. The Light Beings carried flaming torches which illuminated the starry night.

We began to sing, *Kalagaya*, which is the Call to enter Shamballa. As we sang, everyone joined in until the sound echoed and grew to a magnificent crescendo of resonance. Overlapping layers of *Kalagaya* sang throughout the mountains. Then large, golden bells hidden within the mountaintops rang out and merged with our song. Finally, a Golden Sun Disc began to gong with our song as the bells pealed forth and the Call ever expanded...

Looking at one another in amazement, we discovered that we too, were wearing the white and gold ceremonial robes and Lama hats with glowing discs of AN. Then a dazzling Light Being, brighter than any I have encountered before, came through the doorway and greeted us. Crying, we bowed deeply and prostrated ourselves upon the ground. The chanting changed to "Kumari–Kumara, this we be. For the Seven have become the Seventy Seven."

Next, we were led inside the massive doorway to a

crystal pyramid where a vastly radiant Light Being welcomed us with much love. Then the apex of the pyramid opened up, as a shaft of brilliant, piercing Light from the Great Central Sun descended and penetrated us seven times. I felt this in my physical body as powerful jolts of electrical current which caused me to jump violently each time I was struck.

Soon, a large golden crown appeared. It was a ring-pass-not, ever changing. Sometimes it lay flat upon the ground, then it would roll upright, standing on its edge with us inside. Rolling over and over again until it conveyed us to the top of the mountain where we found ourselves inside yet another crystal pyramid.

Inside this pyramid was the Abyss. Standing on the edge, we gazed out into the void's bottomless expanse. Far below we could see twinkling stars. On the far side was a waterfall flowing downwards into the Abyss. I saw large white birds that wanted to fly us across, but somehow that seemed too easy.

My friend suggested that we beam golden strands of Light across the Abyss from our AN discs in our hats. As we did, the strands attached themselves to a tree on the far side and rapidly wove themselves into a golden suspension bridge which we then crossed. Passing by the tree on the far side, we were told to each take a large, globe shaped golden fruit which would serve us later.

Proceeding on our journey, we entered an arched doorway into a round sphere. Carved white seats encircled the inside of this cavern like chamber. In the center stood a large round table composed of a solid piece of quartz crystal. We had entered the intermediate level of the Starry Brotherhood of the Og-Min. I had not known of the existence of this level until now. Inside the chamber were many Light Beings wearing robes similar to ours; some were white and some yellow.

The Og-Min spoke to us, "We are the Keepers of Sacred Time, holding the axis of this planet in Balance."

A Golden Beam pierces the center of the crystal table like a vertical thread, extending through the room. This is the same Golden Beam which passes through the center of the planet like a spindle, keeping it on its rotational axis. This thread extends all the way to Beyond the Beyond. The Golden Beam is also a navigational tracking device, useful for journeys through black holes and spiral galaxies. It emanates a pulsating frequency to keep on track.

When we left the intermediate chambers of the Og-Min, we discovered ourselves to be outside, standing on the perimeter of a square rose garden. Light Beings dressed in iridescent robes of liquid Light, beckoned us to follow them into the center of the garden where there is a crystal Tower of Light.

Inside the Tower, it is delicately beautiful. Starlights are hung on the walls in luminescent brackets etched with exquisite tracery designs. A graceful, golden spiral staircase leads upward.

The radiant Light Beings help us remove our heavy ceremonial robes and we find ourselves garbed in transparent robes of liquid Light. Under our hats, we discover golden headbands with a multi-faceted lotus crystal that is a real star! *These are our starry gifts.*

A Golden Chalice is presented. Dipping our fingers into it, we anoint ourselves with a sacredness of Purpose. Golden Light fills our beings and extends out of our fingertips, toes, crown chakras and eyes. We are streaming forth Golden Light, like rays of the Central Sun.

Then with great effort, as the energies are overwhelmingly powerful, we ascend the spiral stairway. With our last bit of conscious awareness, we enter the chamber of the Council of the One and merge into the Great Light . . . .

At this point, we could continue no further and sank down upon our mats in the back of the van. For a time we lost consciousness completely. Then we slowly sat up, and with the aid of flashlights, wrote down notes of our experiences so they would not be forgotten.

The following day we again spent hiking the mountains, going to a pure, little lake where I waded out to a small island. Here I spied some rocks away from shore that called me forth. Sitting on the rocks, I gazed at the pristine beauty of the Tetons with profound gratitude. Suddenly all the mountains started swirling around, first in one direction and then in another. I became so dizzy that I had to lie down.

Later that afternoon, we activated the Beacon of AN, and made our departure from these magical mountains.

The EL*AN*RA

EL*AN*RA represents the three control points located in the belt of Orion.

These three stars are the pins which keep this dimensional universe into position. Each of these control points contains a specific energy pattern or vibratory frequency chosen to set the keynotes for the establishment and evolution of this dimensional universe which contains myriad patterns of insets and overlays.

The first energy sequence is that of the EL. This corresponds to the first star in Orion's belt, Mintaka. It is also directly aligned with the star system of Arcturus. The EL Essence gave birth to the Elder lineage which long served upon Earth, although no pure ELs remain here today. However, there are many Hybrid-ELs incarnate who keep the EL energy anchored at all times. Hybrid-ELs are those who have merged the EL Essence with other star lineages in order to step down and soften the energy emanation. In times past, pure ELs served upon this planet as great Masters.

The EL energy alignment emphasizes empowered knowledge, the Higher Mind, the dream / mind body, and the will. Interestingly enough, Mintaka is the star from which J. J. Hurtak received the *Keys of Enoch.*

The EL's symbol is the All-Seeing Eye, for they have the ability to align their energies into the collective unconscious as One Mind.

The ELs have long been keepers of the Great Mysteries. They have tremendous intelligence as well as full access into the Akashic Chronicles. ELs were extremely active during the time of Atlantis. They have often served on Earth in positions of leadership and power. Cyclops were early forerunners of the ELs. The color of the EL emanation is blue. It is aligned with the energy of Isis and the Moon. EL energy is presently anchored in Europe, the Atlantic Ocean, the Caribbean, Aegean & Mediterranean Seas.

Δ

The second control point is that of AN. The middle star in Orion's belt, Al Nilam, is the star of AN. AN is directly aligned with the double stargate of Antares and represents the Sun and Moon united as One Being.

AN represents the completion of duality, being both the dreamer and the dream. When the dreamer dances awake his dream, the full potential of this central point is realized and the black hole is not only entered, but transcended.

The ancient civilizations of the Druids, Incas & Egyptians were founded by those of the AN lineage. In all of these, there was a joint rulership by husband and wife who were also brother and sister. They worshiped the Sun and Moon not only as their Gods, but as their true parents. The color of AN is magenta symbolizing the completion of the rainbow when red and purple, the opposite ends of the spectrum representing Sun & Moon, are united. Horus, the offspring of the union between Isis and Osiris, would be a child of AN. The symbol of AN is the sun disc above a crescent moon. And AN's present physical anchoring is in South America.

Δ

The third energy frequency is that of the RA. It is connected to the third star in Orion's belt called Al Nitak.

The RA lineage emanates from the star system of Sirius. Due to Sirius' experience transforming from red sun to white star, they are the overseers of the coming shift in Solar Rulership which will deeply affect our solar system.

The RA emanation is that of the receptive, the dream, intuition, sensual physicality and love. Although it may seem strange that RA contains qualities that are more lunar in nature, its symbol is the Sun. This is because on this level, frequencies are reversed. From RA originate the starry dophins and whales who send their brethren to Earth in order to aid humanity. Those of the RA lineage have often served as priests and mystics. RA is connected to Osiris and Lemuria. It is currently anchored in the islands of Polynesia and the Pacific Ocean.

Δ

The significance of the three control points of EL*AN*RA to the people on Earth cannot be overstated. Until the recent Realignment

of the Stars, they have been the predominate influence upon us. This is now in the process of changing. As we move off the dimensional spiral, their influence shall wane until it has been transcended completely.

The EL*AN*RA is our key to liberating ourselves from duality, for encoded within them are the access points to achieving triangulation. Each of us has an intimate alignment with at least one of the EL*AN*RA. And we must integrate and merge with all three control points before we are ready to ascend to the Template of Oneness. This is an important step in our quest for wholeness and freedom.

And I might add, that as Star-Borne, many of you have had strong experiences with the three magical stars in the belt of Orion. I know that all my life when viewing the starry sky, I always seek them out, feeling a great sense of reassurance that they are still present.

Triangulation

Triangulation is the key to completing duality.

In order to become free from the spheres of duality, we do not step out of it as previously thought. Instead we expand it, thus leading to its completion and transformation. This is achieved by creating a third point. This third point exists above or *beyond* the linear patterning of duality. Once this point is established, a massive activation takes place whereupon a triangle of Light is created, stretching duality into a new, more expanded frequency patterning. This is the process of Triangulation.

There is a correspondence with the awakening of the spiritual centers within the human brain. It begins when the pituitary and pineal glands are activated, thus activating the medulla oblongata within the brain. The medulla oblongata or alta major center is the link between the kundalini energy of the spinal column and the head centers. When it is activated, a process of synergetic triangulation results. This creates the imperishable body of fire. Alice Bailey mentions this process in several of her books.

Possibly we should refer to this as tri-*angel*-ation, because, once again, the Golden Solar Angels hold the key. For they represent the third point that we must bring into manifestation. This apex of the triangle could more accurately be called the *Starry Overself*. It represents conscious union with your vaster Self who is finally embodying on the physical.

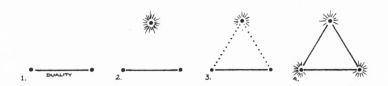

Once triangulation has been achieved and fully activated into the world of matter, you will discover that you have made a quantum leap breakthrough in consciousness, thus opening the door to new levels of liberation from duality.

As increasing numbers of us embody Oneness, we activate the apex of the triangle through *harmonic resonance*, thereby lessening the rule of duality as our predominant reality upon this planet.

Thus shall the process of triangulation further intensify. Duality will no longer be confined to a limited, linear form of expression. Rather it will be loosened to expand beyond its previous boundaries, weaving itself into a New Matrix. This graduation from duality is a prerequisite for the liberation of humanity.

The principles of triangulation were understood and utilized in ancient Egypt. This was symbolized on their circular crowns containing both a vulture and cobra, symbolizing the two cosmic poles. Through the establishment of the Egyptian energy focus, a third point was activated, achieving the state of triangulation. The geometry of the pyramids represents this triangular energy activation.

The Great Pyramids at Giza set the keynote for our entire cycle of earthly evolution under the Template of Duality which we are now completing. Pyramids have been found scattered about the planet to aid in our process of remembrance. Therefore, they have been the most important existing edifices on this planet. Their time is coming to an end which is why they are finally crumbling away. The same could be said for the Sphinx, a solar lion, who is the loyal guardian of the ancient starry mysteries.

Within the geometry of the Great Pyramids is our key to the remembrance of triangulation. Our internal cellular memory banks contain everything needed to decode the imprints of our Divine origins preserved for us upon this planet in pyramidal form.

Another physical manifestation on Earth which is of major importance is the Black Cube of Mecca, called the Kaaba. The Kaaba was placed here long ago by Heavenly Beings under the leadership of Archangel Gabriel in order to anchor the planet into duality. It was originally white, but became black due to the sins of mankind. It will be interesting to see how our transformation into Oneness shall affect these ancient anchors of duality.

No-Time and
the Zone of Silence

The choice is up to you; it always has been. You can either continue life the way you have been living it, or you can choose to transcend duality and move your consciousness up another octave into Oneness, thus flinging open the doors to the Greater Reality.

Herein is the place of No-Time where time stands still and a crack between the worlds opens up, revealing the deep, penetrating Zone of Silence. This is the place of revelation, the place of access to all-knowingness, the entrance hall to the *Greater Reality*.

Some of you have already entered the state of No-Time. You can recognize it when time appears to stand still and stretch open. An instant becomes forever— an eternal moment which contains everything in an endless expanse of open space. Within the Zone of Silence you shall hear the fullest Silence you have ever experienced, containing all sounds united within the eloquent symphony of the *Song of One*. A state of great peace descends and envelops you. You are Home. You are whole. This is the true present which contains both past and future blended into the timeless Now.

Sometimes these experiences are triggered by meditation or by being alone in nature. A good method is to sit quietly and watch the sun setting over the horizon. This can be done either at the ocean or by watching the sun descend behind a mountain. Gaze silently at the sun, slightly squinting your eyes. You should start to see interesting colors and patterns, possibly visions. As the sun begins to descend out of sight, watch carefully for the moment when a line of dazzling Light opens up on the distant horizon. This is the crack between the worlds. If you are ready, you can enter it and go into the Zone of Silence.

At other times it will manifest itself as a deep hush that descends upon you. All conversation ceases. You pause in the midst of a thought or a word, sometimes staring blankly into space. My mother always told me that these moments were caused by Angels passing overhead. When this happens, be still and open yourself to the Zone of Silence.

After you become increasingly familiar with the state of No-Time and the Zone of Silence, you will be able to enter there often.

You can choose to bask in the Silence to heal and renew yourself. Or you can receive access to higher dimensional wisdom. This is the realm of many Greater Mysteries hidden to unawakened humanity. It is also a place to reconnect with Essence. Many find it an inspired base for creation, be it by writing, art, music, dance or whatever form of expression you choose. All you need do is develop the capability to open yourself and listen, for that is the key to receiving. And within the Zone of Silence, all can be heard.

Eventually, you will develop the mastery to *Stop Time* by yourself and move with fluid ease through the myriad dimensional worlds into the Greater Reality. The step after that is to live each moment of your lives anchored within the timeless instant of No-Time. Then you are truly integrated into Oneness.

Panachön

Panachön is the *Ixmat* of Antares. He is not only the guardian of Antares' double stargate, but he *is* the stargate. I first encountered him a few years ago while living in Mount Shasta, California. Often during the summer's nights, my attention would be drawn to a bright star which twinkled at me in recognition. Finally, I looked up this star on my star maps to discover that it was Antares.

One night during an evening meditation on the roof, a long tunnel opened up between me and Antares. The tunnel appeared to be breathing and alive. It somewhat resembled the trunk of an elephant. Passing rapidly through this tunnel, I finally arrived at Antares. There I was greeted by tall, elegant beings with elongated heads, like the early Mayans and Egyptians. Their leader was Panachön.

I felt great love for these kindred beings who welcomed me with obvious joy and respect. In the center of Panachön's forehead was a large mirror disc. As he aligned his mirror disc with mine, *apparently I had one too*, we began to communicate. Many times did I visit Panachön and others on Antares. Here I was shown and taught a great deal. I discovered that the great Ptah was the previous *Ixmat*; and that in order to travel through the double stargate, you enter Panachön's mirror disc. . .

Panachön Speaks:

•
•   •

These dots are codes, as well as the patterns of our star.

All the patterns of the constellations are *encoded dot matrices* which correspond with those already imprinted deep within your cellular memory banks. The purpose of these encoded matrices is to expand your vortices, stretching the parameters of the openings, thus allowing the necessary expansion and anchoring of your vast Starry Overselves.

These Starry Overselves are not solely a personal matter. Once you cease to identify totally as an individualized unit of consciousness, you enter a *Zone of Overlap.* This Zone of Overlap is composed of *Merged Love Essence,* the fabric of the Greater Reality.

We call you to enter this Zone of Merged Essence which could also be termed the Zone of Oneness. When you have expanded into your Starry Overselves, you are no longer anchored within the confines of duality. Your Starry Overself emanates from beyond the parameters of duality and has already merged with the One.

The journey is simple and uncomplicated. Yet, many have strived and yearned, but failed to find the key. They have attempted to make this transformation without surrendering the concept of themselves as separate units of consciousness.

Many have also confused mindlessness with No-Mind, which is a state of open surrender. As we let go of our old mental processes, a new state of No-Mind serves as an open door to the Invisible and receives total access to the One.

Within the Invisible reigns pristine clarity, a deep inner peace and a sense of complete fulfillment. Enhanced frequencies of Love become the very air we breathe, the core substance of every molecule. This is what we have all yearned to experience.

After we have received a taste of Oneness, we desire increasingly deeper immersions within it, until finally we anchor into the Invisible, becoming embodiments of Oneness. Our beings no longer experience the illusion of separation, for we now reside in the One Heart.

The One Heart is an ocean of Love. We are composed of these watery, starry currents as is the very air about us. This is living, breathing, pulsating Love Essence. It is all around—within us and without us. We need not search or yearn. Simply be still and acknowledge what is right here, right now—in its fullness and depth, in its vast multi-dimensionality, in its timeless eternity.

Float upon this current of deep peace, of purest Love, of Silence which containeth all sounds. Flow and you shall fly, for here freedom abounds. We are unlimited. We are united in Oneness. We are unbound, caressed by pulsating waves of All Encompassing Love, the Light frequency of Essence.

Here True Love prevails,
the most exquisite music of all,
the Song of One.

Realignment of the Stars

One of the major effects of Earth Link in February 1988 was the commencement of the Realignment of the Stars.

This is of great significance and its effects are only beginning to become apparent. What this means is that planet Earth is being influenced by entirely new star patternings than we have experienced before. These emerging new star patternings are still in their stage of infancy, but shall increasingly grow in importance with time.

There is a steady shifting in the heavens which is causing profound changes. As you know, space is not flat. It curves and bends, containing pockets and folds within it. These pockets and folds are currently in the process of moving. Thus we shall discover that unknown star fields, previously hidden in folds in space or secreted in sealed pockets, are now slowly being revealed.

Conversely, many star field frequency patternings to which Earth has long been accustomed, are slowly being withdrawn.

They are being recalled into newly created pockets and folds in deep space. This is of tremendous importance. It is part of the new Divine Dispensation and is a pre-requisite for the establishment of the new etheric blueprint and grid matrix overlay.

Some of these changes have already begun to be observed in the night sky by our astronomers, since the Realignment of the Stars actually began long ago. It has simply taken this long for the changes to be visible to us due to the slow speed that Light travels. In the meantime, while we wait for science to catch up to metaphysics to supply the physical "proof" which some people require, we are already being affected by this shift.

We can experience this influx of new star field energies as part of the heightened acceleration of these times.

They are helping to bring in the heightened frequencies which are aiding our process of restructurization and recalibration. They will assume an even greater importance as we move into the New Octave which we term the Seventh Star. This is where we make the quantum leap into Oneness.

Now, as we prepare our Homeward Vehicle, leaving behind our illusory identification of ourselves as individualized units of consciousness, we are being called forth into Oneness by the Song of Stars. Likewise, as our old third dimensional patterning drops away, this is accompanied by the withdrawal of old star fields which served to keep us locked into duality. All this is in perfect accord with the Divine Plan.

Anchoring the New Star Fields

The entrance of new star fields has begun. . .

A few of them have already been anchored on Earth. Some of you have important work to do in this regard. If you are connected with anchoring new star fields, you will recognize this, just be reading these words. Right about now, you should be experiencing a profound tingling inside your body. Many have chosen to serve this task, most often with star fields that you are quite familiar with. Some of these you have thought of as Home. You came to Earth in order to serve as their anchoring pinions. It should be most exciting, now that the time has finally arrived.

Most of the preliminary anchoring will take place between now and 1992 preparing for the Activation of the 11:11, although the work will continue in an altered manner until the end of 2011. The reason for this timing schedule should become apparent by the time you complete this book. It has to do with the movement of the Birdstar through the Doorway of the 11:11.

In June 1988, a new star field called Oriolon Fanatrix was anchored in the mountains north of Los Angeles, California. It emanates a refined Golden frequency which, in time, will greatly alter that area by transforming it into a center of creativity.

Another new star field named Aragon was anchored off the coast of Oregon in December 1988. Closely aligned with A·Qua·La A·Wa·La who is spoken of next in these pages, Aragon is birthing new vortexes for healing both the oceans and our emotions. A small group of dedicated beings are working closely with these energies. Aragon is aqua in color.

The star field of Ogatta was anchored in early 1992, coinciding with the 11:11 Activation. This is significant since Ogatta is located in the tip of the beak of our Birdstar. The Birdstar represents a new star overlay necessary in order to create the vehicle of our Unified Presence for our homeward journey. It corresponds with pre-ordained star patternings encoded into our cellular memory banks prior to our descent into matter. When Ogatta was activated it enabled us to access and retrieve much that we had long forgotten. This heralded a new level of remembrance.

Many other new star fields will be anchored in the days to come. Some of you are deeply connected with this process and even now, are making the necessary preparations for the entry of your star field. You have carried their names around with you for a long time, yet until the present moment did not recognize what their purpose was. Your cellular memory banks have hereby been activated that you may now read sealed orders which have resided within you for aeons. For the time has come.

A·Qua·La ∴ A·Wa·La

I was meditating one night while living on the coast of Oregon when a beautiful Starry Being appeared whom I had never before seen. She was so vast that her feet were in the ocean and her head amongst the stars. Her name is A·Qua·La A·Wa·La and she is the Elohim of the Oceans and Healer of Emotions. Her long blonde hair was sprinkled with tiny white seashells and her aqua robes were tinged with iridescent sparkles of magenta, gold, lavender and blue.

A·Qua·La A·Wa·La is new to this planet and resides on the same octave as the Bodhisattva Kuan Yin. In fact, she is like a sister to Kuan Yin, the Bodhisattva of Love, Mercy & Compassion. Kuan Yin's emanation is rose while A·Qua·La A·Wa·La's is aqua. She is here to help us heal our emotions and our oceans. The first part of her name corresponds with the dolphins while the second part is aligned with the whales—for they could be said to be her people. Together, they serve to balance our emotions.

Since A·Qua·La A·Wa·La is not separate from us, but is her Essence is found within us, her healing

Presence is available whenever needed. I am delighted to discover that such a remarkable one is here to aid us in anchoring the One Heart. It's like fresh troops coming in to heal us from our travails, that we may complete our cycle of service and prepare for ascension into the Template of Oneness.

Before I moved from Oregon, several of her crystal pyramids had been activated, as well as some awakened beings who now anchor and embody her Essence, that we may bring emotional healing to humanity and the entire planetary body.

As you read the following messages from her, I hope that you will be able to experience the wondrous healing nourishment of her radiant Essence.

I Am A•Qua•La .˙. A•Wa•La:

I am here walking among you in order to prepare for the new Divine Dispensation. Never before have I appeared among you, though long have I watched over you.

I am the Elohim of the Waters, the Guardian of your Oceans, the Healer of Emotions. I have come to heal, to bring renewal, to prepare for your rebirth into the New Octave.

I now appear on the coastlines of your great oceans for this is where I am most needed. The shores of Aragon have long been prepared for my coming. There is a purity and serenity here which enables me to manifest my Essence unto those of you who would listen and who would see.

I am the Essence of Liquid, be it Light or Water or Emotions, traveling here upon the subtle currents of the starry oceans. In truth, like you, I am a Star.

It is important to remember that you are composed of aqueous substance. The tides of your emotions rise and fall as do the tides of Earth's oceans. I am here to heal your emotions, to bring them into balance, to birth your new emotional body and to anchor the One Heart.

This shall be achieved by immersing you within the deep Sea of Love wherein resides the One Heart. As this All Encompassing Love permeates your being, your subtle aqueous currents shall begin to flow in harmony with the Greater Reality. The Essence of your being shall merge into the One Heart until no vestige of separation remains. Your emotions will be smoothed and soothed by the Celestial Harmonies, flowing effortlessly into the New Octave.

Hence you shall feel more, not less. These new emotions emanate from the place of all-knowing, all-feeling—All Encompassing Love resonating in harmony with the pure Essence of the One Heart. Such an alignment will be liberating to a degree you cannot yet imagine.

Remember that the polluted oceans of earth simply mirror the pollution of your emotional bodies. By cleansing one, we shall purify the other. Let us begin within.

For this purpose, I have created eleven crystal pyramids off the coast of Aragon. I did this by loosening my necklace of crystalline beads. Each of these beads contains the concentrated Essence of the One Heart. I have caused eleven of these beads to fall to Earth, each one of them landing in quiet coves pre-ordained for their arrival long ago. Here they have quickly transformed into pyramids of Light.

The purpose of these pyramids is not only to stabilize your coastlines, which is being done, but to stabilize your emotions as well. For in these times of ever accelerating frequencies, emotions are often the first area to weaken under stress. Hence these stabilization pinions are most helpful.

I am A·Qua·La A·Wa·La. I walk among you with vast Love. I am not separate from you, although you may initially perceive me to be. I am within each of you—as each of you is within me.

As my feet rest within the watery oceans of your planet, my body extends all the way into the Invisible. My entire radiant being forms a pathway of liquid, starry Love. Truly, there is no more separation between what is above and what is below.

Remember: Each drop contains within it the Love of the One. Each drop yearns to return to the One Heart. Each of you is making that homeward journey right now.

Simply surrender and flow. . .

I Am A • Qua • La ∴ A • Wa • La:

The waters do smooth out,
the emotions doth calm.
Yet, now you see
how it is meant to be
in these tumultuous times.

No longer manifesting in linear,
no thread of logic running through,
balance is entirely up to you.
Everything chaotically changing.
The unexpected reigns
upon the seas of life.

The internal center of focus
must be found and maintained
regardless of what appears without.
Your being must be anchored
constantly within the One Heart.

Keep the sound of silence
echoing throughout your heart.
Always remember who you are,
that you are beautiful and worthy,
that you are holy and wise.

Walk in love upon your path,
embody your magnificent Truth.
Be nothing less nor nothing more.
Above all, simply be Love.

I Am A·Qua·La.˙.A·Wa·La:

The etheric crystal pyramids off the coast of Aragon are presently being readied for full activation. This is to augment and reinforce the grid overlay system of the New Matrix, thereby strengthening and stabilizing those zones currently undergoing great stress and pressure.

It is important to remember that both the planetary tectonic plate system and the grid systems are in the process of tremendous change. Soon, both of these systems will be obsolete as this planet lifts into a New Star Matrix.

During this time of changeover and transformation, the inherent stress factor is greater than usual. Utmost caution must be exercised; this is why many have been called to higher frequency octaves to assist in stabilizing the planetary energies during this momentous transition. Some of you have experienced unaccustomed sluggishness and a sense of disconnection with the third dimension while aiding us in this project.

We could describe this grid shift to you as both a lifting up and a laying down. The lifting up is of the old tectonic plate and grid systems. Once they are lifted, a new encoding is superimposed upon the existing system. This interweaving of the old with the new creates the mandalic patterning of the New Star Matrix. This is a somewhat delicate maneuver requiring the help and participation of many.

To return to the coastal pyramids, there are eleven of them placed along the coast of Aragon. Once activated, they shall serve as Light Beacons, stabilizing the coastline until the new Dispensation takes effect. They are similar to accupressure points upon the planet which, as activated, shall serve to move the planetary emotional body into the frequency zone of the One Heart.

A Healing

I am A·Qua·La A·Wa·La and I come to offer you the gift of emotional healing. It is most important at this time that this healing be done in order to move onward into the New Octave which awaits.

Come with me on a journey into the starry oceans of the Greater Reality. Take this time out for yourself, for you deserve the nourishment that true healing brings. Sit quietly and read this slowly, for we are going to travel beyond time to the place where deep inner peace prevails and Love is all embracing.

Let me take your hand and lead you there. We shall begin by walking slowly along the shore of the Sea of Oneness. This ocean is a soothing azure blue, sparkling with sprinkles of tiny stars. It stretches out endlessly to a far distant horizon that cannot be seen, for this is the timeless Ocean of Eternity. Hand in hand we shall walk together upon the crystalline shore. Above us are the vast Celestial Heavens filled with our Starry Brethren. The air is fresh and clear, allowing us to breathe deeply and freely.

A profound sense of silent wonder fills your being as you experience new depths of serenity. Never before have you felt so calm and protected. The waves break onto the shore with an enduring timelessness. We stand quietly observing the waves steadily flowing in and out.

And now we walk into the waves, stepping slowly and carefully into the water. You discover that the water is warm and relaxing, welcoming you ever deeper. We begin to swim effortlessly, carried along by the undulating currents of the starry sea. Your entire being is filled with delight at the ease and pleasure of riding the rolling waves. Laughter bubbles up inside of you and is joyously expressed.

Suddenly up pops a glistening dolphin who has been called to your side by the sound of your delight. Upon his face is a wide open smile, welcoming you to his watery realms. Climbing aboard his back, you embrace him as he takes you down to the watery depths. You discover that you can breathe as well underwater as you can upon the surface. And together you glide through layers and layers of crystalline liquid sea, down to the place where true healing resides.

Here I await you, in the fullness of my Presence, surrounded by my whale and dolphin brethren. We are in the central chamber of the One Heart where True Love prevails. You are immersed in waves upon waves of All Encompassing Love. I hand you a chalice of aquamarine liquid filled with the Essence of True Love. This sacred elixir has been specially prepared to heal your heart, to smooth and soothe away your sorrows, to mend your broken hearts, to lighten your weariness and to melt away your fears.

Drink deeply my beloved one, for the time has come for you to be thoroughly healed. As you put the aqua elixir into your mouth, you experience a warm sensation of profound nourishment. You feel it travel throughout your body, healing wherever the need exists. Bringing a gentle breeze of Love which tingles your insides, causing you to surrender into joyous delight.

The old careworn sadness instantly dissolves into a new sense of wholeness and empowered Love which radiates from your eyes and heart. You feel filled with Truest Love—loving everyone, everything, and most especially, loving yourself. You discover that Love is easy, not difficult as you had always assumed. Love is as easy and natural as breathing! Love is as all-pervasive as the water which surrounds you.

And within this magical moment of revelation, you choose Love! You choose Love for the entire universe, for our galaxy, for the solar system, for the planet Earth, for all humanity. And you choose Love for yourself! For we all deserve to be ever embraced in the arms of Love. It's the natural order of the One. And it's always around us, all we have to do is to recognize it.

The dolphins are so happy to be bathed in the radiance of your Loving Presence that they begin a delightful dance, churning up the waters until they are filled with starry foam. You dance with the dolphins, somersaulting in starry spirals of bubbling currents which take you ever upwards until you arrive on the calmly undulating surface of the Ocean of Eternity.

Here you emerge—cleansed, healed, renewed and recalibrated. Now you are ready to enter the New Octave which awaits . . .

The Homeward Journey

The New Octave

We are now within the process of shifting into a New Octave of Oneness.

This can be visualized as moving from a visible spiral into a greater spiral located within the Invisible. While we are making this adjustment, much of what we have previously known begins to disappear as we turn to a vaster vantage point.

Our vibratory frequency is altering to a new harmonic patterning. Thus much of what has previously vibrated in accord with us no longer resonates. Some of our previous knowledge will remain during the transitional phase, for this will be a gradual cessation of all we've previously known and experienced.

A lesser type of frequency shift happened when we moved from the ancient energy focus to the Angelic frequency. Remember how much of what had previously interested and fulfilled us, that we held sacred—no longer pertained, as if it had suddenly become lifeless. The same thing is happening now on a much vaster scope. We are being freed from the old as we complete our old level of awareness.

Please do not worry or despair over what you are letting go. A vast surrendering of old energy patterns is most appropriate at this time. As we move into higher realms of consciousness, we will notice that some of

our old friends will be able to vibrate in accord with these new frequencies, while others will not. Of course, we will constantly meet new beings with whom we can resonate in harmony.

Remember that we are the forerunners, the explorers into the Invisible who shall make the path easier for others to find. This means that we will constantly be called to travel through new thresholds of consciousness. Some are not yet ready to enter these doorways, having chosen other areas of experience. Hence, what appears to be a separation between you shall take place. This is really more a completion than a separation—both a merger and a releasing. Let them go with Love. Let go of those parts of yourself and your life which no longer serve your Highest Truth. They have been completed. Move on to the New Octave which awaits.

There is more than one soul group or star family that we belong to. They exist on myriad dimensional levels. As we grow and lighten, we will refine our beings to draw higher frequency star lineages into our sphere.

Although we are as yet, uncertain and unfamiliar with the New Octave, increasingly shall it be revealed. Much which we have striven to shed shall be gone at last. As the new reveals itself, our healed hearts shall sing the song of joyous liberation. And True Love will be fully expressed. The profound holiness of simple joys will be unveiled as we shed our layers of countless cloaks of disguise.

Arise and see. Essence free. Simply be.

I Am Solaris Antari:

The doors are wide open, for a mass activation is in effect. All Light Workers are being placed on full alert. It is time to loosen the bonds of duality in order to step fully into the embodiment of that which You Truly Are.

To achieve this activation, a heightened acceleration, of a degree never before experienced on this planet, is in effect. This massive increase in vibratory acceleration is causing a wobble effect which is loosening the rigid calcification of duality.

You can feel the wobble within your being as your internal vibratory rate increasingly accelerates. You can also feel this wobble inside the planetary body as Earth shakes and lurches along its internal axis. This is for the greater good, although the wobble presents the possibility of greater occurrence of geophysical Earth shifts as well as the proliferation of unstable events.

It would be helpful if you would focus your attention on sending a shaft of Golden Light through the center of the planetary body in order to serve as a stabilization pinion. This activity would also be helpful inside your own being. It will pin you to the Golden Beam while allowing all that is ready to be released, to do so.

You are being drawn to your chosen areas of endeavor. You are being led to those with whom you have chosen to serve, what you refer to as Starry Family.

Respect and serve each other fully with no holding back, for it is now time to engage your energies in the manifestation and embodiment of your Higher Purpose.

The Islands of Light are ready to be established onto the physical plane after having waited in position on the etheric plane for so long. You know who you are. You know what you are here to do. Now simply begin. This period of heightened acceleration will be in effect for some time. Fully utilize these energies and step through the open portals before you.

The time of hindrance is past. All things long yearned for in the depths of your heart will be freely given. Allow yourself to receive them. Allow yourself to believe and trust in the immaculate perfection of the Divine Plan as it manifests within your life.

Allow yourself to go forward, stepping freely out of the bonds of the third and fourth dimensions. The shackles have been loosened. Now it is up to you to remove them in order to experience freedom and fulfillment to a degree previously unimaginable.

The choice is yours whether to answer the Call which resounds across the Celestial Vastness and resonates deep within your

heart. Do not hesitate or you shall miss the accelerated grace of this time.

Please, be courageous and step forward as your Highest Truth. The need is great, for planet Earth stands on the threshold of decision. As do you. The future is being created right now. We have reached the crossroads. The roads between duality and Oneness do fork and separate. Soon it will no longer be possible to straddle them in compromise.

You can tip the balance by your full emergence. The frequency of our Call has been vastly increased in order that many of you might respond to the needs of this time with the magnificence of your full Presence. This commitment must be made and irrevocably anchored within your entire being right now.

The glimpse you have hereby been given
foretells a merger into the One.
A partition is in position until you are able
to fully integrate the totality of your being.
In reality, this window is but a mirror.
You are looking at Yourself.

All veils to the Greater Reality
have been but an illusion.
You, who have longed to return
to the heart of the One
have been there all along.
You are the All That Is.
The All That Is
 is the One & the Many.
That is you.

The homeward vehicle is hereby being prepared.
It is created by activating our Unified Presence.

It is this One who shall return Home.
Together, united as One,
we are the homeward vehicle.

The first Call to Return has sounded,
signifying the full activation of the Call to Action.
Now is the time to make our Unified Presence
felt upon the Earth.
The Angels are being called
into full, conscious embodiment
as instruments of Divine Intervention
and as anchors of the Golden Beam.

Rising into conscious alignment
with your Starry Overself
is of the highest priority at this time,
since it is a prerequisite for your entrance
into the New Octave which beckons
on the continuing spiral homeward.

Initiation Into Oneness

For our next phase of evolution we must come together as One.

This entails an initiation into Oneness wherein we merge our separate identities on an Essence level and create a new state of collective beingness. In order to facilitate this, we must release our attachment to ourselves as individualized units of consciousness. This is our greatest and final attachment to duality. It is the last portal which must be passed through in order to move into the Greater Reality.

Although we have long known that we are One in Essence, we have still clung onto our identification with ourselves as separate entities. This has been entirely appropriate and necessary during our cycle of Earth experiences in the Template of Duality. It was in perfect harmony with the Divine Plan that we perceive ourselves as separate from each other so we could fully develop our state of awakened *conscious* Oneness.

However, to move onward into the New Octave, we must now lovingly release our identification as separate beings.

You may discover within yourself a whole new set of fears about letting go of this final illusion. You may feel that if you do this you will cease to exist. But this is not the case; you will actually be more alive and vital, more fulfilled and radiating than ever before. And you will be much closer to the state of being which we call Home.

Oneness does not mean that we are all the same. We still bring our unique combination of energy to our star of One. It does means that our predominant reality shifts from being separate individuals to being part of a greater whole. Once again, we are venturing into the realms of the Unknown. Here we shall experience an enhanced state of beingness as we unite into One vast Being. As our primary identification with ourselves as individualized units of consciousness fades away, we shall become larger, not smaller.

Our collective being is immensely vaster and more magnificent than anything we can presently imagine. Together as One, we can achieve that which we have most yearned for during our phase as separate beings. We will experience true fulfillment. This is a prerequisite for completion upon the earthplane.

Hence we are being called upon to make the final sacrifice, which shall prove to be no sacrifice at all. We are called to unite together in an initiation into Oneness, merging the family of humanity into a collective whole. Our primary identifications with ourselves shall be with the One which we truly are— you, me, and everyone else combined.

This is the quantum leap which leads us ever closer to Home!

Islands of Light

We hereby urge you to gather together to form Islands of Light.

These shall be scattered communities throughout the world in which we will join together with others of our Starry Family in order to serve as anchors of the Greater Reality. For we are finally ready to come together with full recognition that we are One.

These Islands of Light shall be perceived as colonies of awakened beings united in the One Heart. Here we will be able to live openly together as Starry Family, birthing new ways of sacred living, embodying new frequencies of Love while anchoring the Invisible into the physical.

Once created and established, our combined Islands of Light shall form one vast mandala of Golden Light which will encircle and embrace the entire Earth.

As this mandala expands into its full radiance, it will align with the Golden Grid causing a heightened activation which further strengthens the New Matrix.

A few of these communities have already been

established, others are in their beginning stages. Most are waiting to be found and created. All Islands of Light must be established and activated soon to serve as stabilization pinions during the shift from duality to Oneness.

If you feel called to become part of an Island of Light, but have not yet found your place and your people, do not worry. Everything will be revealed within its proper timing.

Before we can live in an Island of Light, we must become firmly anchored in Oneness.

In the meantime, you can occupy yourself with completing all unfinished business and unresolved relationships in your present location. Hence, you will be free to move quickly when you are led to your place.

Some might discover a connection with more than one Island of Light and will be traveling on a consistent basis between two or more areas. Many will be happily settled in one location. Others will find that their area of service requires living outside of their chosen community, while maintaining close links with it.

Each person drawn to an Island of Light shall bring an immensely needed gift. It will be the gift of your being as well as useful talents and skills to share with others. For those who have chosen to acquire monetary wealth, your form of service may be to help purchase the land and supply building materials.

Once all our Islands of Light are anchored into position, we will move into a New Octave of collective Oneness, weaving ourselves into the New Matrix. Our magnificent Islands of Light shall serve not only as the seeds of our future, but as launching points of ascension into ever deeper realms of Oneness.

The Seventh Star is born,
It's time for the new dawn!

This is the entrance into the New Octave.

The New Octave awaits those who are ready to step beyond their previous boundaries. It is an expansion of consciousness into spheres of awareness where only Oneness exists and we are merely concentrations of pure love energy, where we can be perceived as pulsations of Light frequencies merged into One Heart.

The Seventh Star is born. In this state, we are formless, beingless, nothing and everything combined. This is Home. This is what we have long yearned for, although now all yearnings have ceased. We are dissolved in sacred merger with the One Heart.

The birth of the Seventh Star foretells a time in which small groups of humanity shall greatly accelerate their homeward process.

As we shed our cloaks of individuality and merge

together as One Being, our Unified Presence shall serve to sustain and anchor the Seventh Star upon Earth.

The Seventh Star is first birthed within the heavens, then it is anchored into the Earth. This is happening right now. The purpose of the Seventh Star is to usher in a New Octave of *conscious* Oneness in order to greatly quicken the ascension of Earth and its myriad life forms into the Greater Reality. It signals the end of the phase in which humanity's primary identification has been as individualized units of consciousness and the completion of the Template of Duality.

The Seventh Star derives from dimensions five through seven which leadeth to eleven. It heralds the movement *beyond* the dimensional patterning of duality. It emanates from the realms of the Invisible.

The Birdstar could be said to be the emissary of the Seventh Star, though this is not entirely accurate, for the Birdstar is also the symbolic representation of our Unified Presence.

By uniting our Angelic Selves together in Oneness and aligning our Starry Overselves into the One Heart, we birth the Seventh Star and the Birdstar returns.

With the birth of the Seventh Star comes the full activation of the Birdstar. All of this knowledge has long been stored within your pre-encoded cellular memory banks awaiting its moment of activation and retrieval. Such a moment has come.

The Seventh Star is reached through the Doorway of the 11:11. It is birthed by the Three and anchored by the Four. It manifests through the Six. The Seventh Star is the crown jewel in the Crown of the Eleven.

The Seventh Star represents the Initiation into the Invisible. It dissolves all artificial

barriers which have held into position the illusion of separation.

It heralds a reuniting of elements which have long been held apart, signifying a profound restructuring of energy patterns on dimensions three and four. This could be termed a *molecular exchange*. This molecular exchange is made possible due to the Realignment of the Stars now in effect. It is a shifting of molecular patterning allowing the new etheric blueprint to manifest on personal, planetary and universal levels. This is necessary in order to fully position ourselves within the energy field of the Birdstar, our vehicle for the impending ascension into Oneness.

The Seventh Star Has Come!

Calling you to surrender your total being into a New Octave. This is similar to releasing yourself into the churning waters of a whirlpool. You find yourself spiraling rapidly within the energy field of vastness. The electromagnetic pull is stronger than anything you have previously experienced. You are effortlessly sucked into the eye of the vortex, completely letting go of everything.

While you are undergoing the process of being pulled in deeper and deeper, you are also experiencing a massive death of many elements of your being not compatible to your entrance into this New Octave. This explains your emotions of loss and mourning. The parts of you anchored in duality are indeed dying away. You are also undergoing a thorough restructuring and recalibration on deep cellular levels that you may be reborn anew. The seed of the Seventh Star planted within you quickens and triggers full activation of the appropriate pre-encoded cellular memories. When this restructuring process is complete, be prepared to face your future as an entirely new being, for that you shall be.

The Seventh Star is reached through the Doorway of the 11:11. This doorway can be perceived and entered by those who have consciously anchored their Starry Overselves into their physical bodies. The forcefields inherent in the 11:11 require this, hence it is veiled to many. As you look at the map of the 11:11, you can see shifting pulsations of Light frequencies, much like a television satellite weather photo.

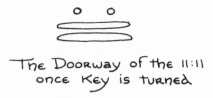

The Doorway of the 11:11
once Key is turned

When the key is turned, the entrance deepens and a corridor is seen while the frequency pulsations continue.

Once entered, the corridor becomes a rapidly coursing runway of Light streaming into the galactic core of the Seventh Star. Here in the galactic core of the Seventh Star is the One Heart. This newly birthed Star emits a vibration of gentle purity. Above a giant pendulum swings back and forth, becoming ever faster and more massive, insistently swinging to and fro with increasing increments of power. This is accompanied by music—forceful, compelling and repetitive, along with the sound of bells, like church bells, pealing and tolling—announcing the birth of the New Octave throughout the many universes.

In the center of the Star something opens, much like the mouth of a starfish, and a delicate white bird is emitted. The small bird spirals up and out through layers of Star, growing ever larger as it flies. By the time it reaches the open heavens, it has become a vast white Birdstar, almost transparent, for stars can be seen through its translucent snowy body.

· This Birdstar is immensely powerful as it flies with fullest authority and empowerment through the starry skies.

· Yet it is composed solely of purest Essence of Love.

· Inside the bird's heart is a seed of the Seventh Star, glowing brilliantly.

· The Birdstar of the Seventh Star flies forth unfettered and free.

· It has full rights of passage to fly where it may throughout the myriad dimensional universes.

· It is stamped with the authority of the One & the Many.

· Within the Birdstar we are One Being, fully merged into Oneness.

· We are on our journey Home.

· The Birdstar has been sent by the Seventh Star to seek us out, to Call us Home, to meld us into One.

· For the journey Homeward is achieved by only One.

Implosion of Duality

The Seventh Star is brought to birth by the Three and anchored by the Four.

The Three can be perceived as three, huge triangular baffles in space, all pointing inwards, but not touching. In the center there is delicate movement, a gentle stirring in the empty stillness. As the baffles remain in position, they begin to activate. They reveal their names which are spoken rapidly in quick succession, causing the triangles of energy to spin around ever faster at dizzying speeds. This causes a spiral starry vortex to gently form in the sacred center space. It is a whirlpool of tiny, shining stars, rippling in the churning currents of space formed by the spinning triangles of energy. Thus is the Seventh Star birthed within the newly formed starry vortex.

You could also say that the Seventh Star has been birthed into the third dimension by the Three. Now it shall be anchored by the Four. These Four are will, knowledge, silence & power. The four elements are anchoring the Seventh Star into the fourth dimension, which also anchors it into the Earth.

As long as the third and fourth dimensions remained separate on Earth, which they did for such a long time, the Seventh Star could not be born. But now through our combined efforts, we have anchored the fourth dimension firmly on this planet. This has caused what we term an *Implosion of Duality* wherein what has long been separate finally reunites. This is similar to the process of nuclear fission and is every bit as powerful.

When the third and fourth dimensions merged during Harmonic Convergence in 1987, this set off an awesome energy force creating the three triangular baffles in space, thus setting into motion the necessary ingredients for birthing the Seventh Star.

The Seventh Star manifests through the Six. This refers to the six dimensions contained within the known universe. As the Seventh Star derives from dimensions five through seven, part of the Seventh Star resides on the other side of the Gateway to the Invisible. This gateway is called the Doorway of the 11:11.

The seventh level or Octave Seven leads to Octave Eleven. When you pass through the Doorway of the 11:11, you arrive at Octave Seven. From here, through a sudden reversal and inversion of direction, you are propelled directly to Octave Eleven. This octave is the launching pad which leads to Beyond the Beyond.

This information is a map detailing the flight of the Birdstar our Homeward Vehicle, created by our Unified Presence as it travels on its homeward journey.

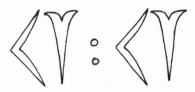

The Doorway of the 11:11

11:11 is the Doorway to the Invisible.

Many of us have been encoded with the seed patterns of the 11:11. This occurred long before our first embodiment upon this planet. When the starseed of the 11:11 is activated, we begin to receive the Call to fully awaken, rise up and start our Homeward Journey.

11:11 has long been our pre-ordained signal that our time of completion is near.

It signifies the beginning of the state of NO-DOWN, NO-RETURN. It is our key to unlock the Portal of Ascension into Oneness. As the 11:11 is activated, the Seventh Star is born and the Birdstar returns.

We are called to quickly take our appointed positions within the massive body of the Birdstar. This must be done in a state of full surrender and total commitment to the One. For we are being Called to serve a far greater Purpose than any of us could achieve on our own. We quicken and enliven the One by taking our positions within the Birdstar. This is vaster and more profound than anything we can yet imagine. The time for us to be predominately perceiving ourselves as individualized units of consciousness is now past. Let the illusion of separation gently dissolve and fade away.

The Doorway of the 11:11 leads to Octave

Seven which takes you to Octave Eleven. Octave Seven is the starting point on the Template of Oneness. It is our new foundation. It is also the staging point to Octave Eleven.

Octave Eleven is what we have sought. This is where we must go, but it is not our final destination. In Octave Eleven, there is a profound shift of Great Central Sun Systems which allows for the entrance of absolutely new frequencies of Love and creative expression. Octave Eleven could also be described as a *launching pad* into spheres of consciousness beyond the imaginable.

The Birdstar is our Homeward Vehicle. The shape of the Birdstar is identical to the pre-ordained star pattern encoded within us long ago. The movement of the Birdstar as it flies is Love in Action. The Birdstar must be quickened by our Unified Presence. Only the unified, complete Birdstar can enter the Doorway of the 11:11. This Doorway must be passed through on the Homeward Journey.

• The Doorway of the 11:11 opens once and closes once. It can be entered by only One.

• Once passed through, there is No-Down, No-Return.

• The 11:11 shall open on January 11th, 1992 and close on December 31st, 2011.

• It will take the full twenty years for the massive body of the Birdstar to complete its passage through the Doorway of the 11:11.

• In Octave Seven the Birdstar inverts into a Starbird to complete the journey to Octave Eleven.

The Dream

On my first night home after traveling, I could not sleep, though I was very tired. In my restlessness, I drew a "Medicine Card" which told me to pay particular attention to my dreams, as I was going to receive a significant dream. This greatly cheered me as it was very late at night, and I was beginning to think that I would have no sleep at all. Soon enough, I fell asleep and this is what I dreamt:

Some of our Starry Family were visiting with a group of holy men from another dimension. The holy men wore long white robes and beards and looked like Sufis. All of them were observing a vow of silence connected with some religious observance, except for their leader who was obviously a great sage. We found ourselves in a place that resembled a small Arab village. Hanging from the bare branches of the trees were long shards of glass tinkling in the breeze like windchimes. We formed a circle with the holy men so that they could enter our sphere, as it was necessary to undergo some sort of energy exchange in order to meld dimensions.

The brotherhood of holy men covered one of our

group's chest with large pieces of orange peel to aid the entry process. All of a sudden, this Angel, who is not easily given to panic, became afraid and announced that we should leave quickly as we might be in danger.

We hurriedly gathered together into our own circle. Once we had formed our circle we were free to depart. But right before we left, their great sage approached and gave me a message of immense importance. As I read it, I realized that I must remember it, so I made myself wake up from my dream and find a pen and paper in order to write down as much as I could. This is what I wrote:

We bear tidings of great importance for you and your planet. We have come to announce that the Time of Completion is near.

We are the Ancient Ones from the Stars. We shall not be able to meet with you like this again, for our sphere shall soon rotate out of the field of contact. We have connected with you at this time in order to deliver this one message. *Now I saw the docking procedure which entailed overlapping two circles, thus forming a central, inner circle where our two spheres or dimensions overlapped and where we had sat together.*

The Light Bearers on Earth are being activated for the planet is currently receiving distorted frequencies emanating from the fourth dimensional astral plane. This is in violation of Cosmic Law. We, ourselves, can do nothing to prevent this. Thus we must withdraw our energies and return to our state of wandering Star Travelers, for we are like nomadic Bedouins of the Stars. We no longer have a home to return to.

We have come to you in peace. We leave you in peace. We are sorry that we have caused you any fear. Although it is not surprising, due to the different frequencies involved in our energy exchange.

The Earth must be alerted through a mass awakening. Little time remains for this, less than three years. Then the Homeward Vehicle, known as the Birdstar, begins its return journey. This journey shall be complete at the end of the Earth year 2011. We urge you to make all necessary adjustments and preparations to get yourself into your proper positions.

Earth shall then experience a profound dimensional shift as the part which ascends into Oneness through the Doorway of the 11:11 irrevocably separates from that which remains in duality. You might say that Earth shall shed her skin. And you would not enjoy the incoming frequency exchange in the fragment of Earth which holds onto the old patterning and therefore cannot go through the Door.

We emanate from Octave Seven, hence shall await you on the other side of the Doorway. There you shall not find us strange.

Until then, make haste and gather your Starry Family together. Be open, yet vigilant. Create your places for the future now. These shall be known as Islands of Light and will become the launching points for ascension wherein you will move with ease into the Greater Reality. This is of utmost importance.

We approach you with love. We leave you in love. We have not meant to frighten you, but merely to warn you that the Time of Completion and Freedom is near.

When you hear the Call to Return, remember not to panic. Instead rise up into your full remembrance and empowerment. Align into One Heart and embody that vast Love to all.

Do not fear for your safety while you are on Earth. Each of you has a strong forcefield of protection which shall remain intact for the duration.

You are placed here in order to serve the All That Is. Now is the time to make your Unified Presence felt!

We go now in love. . .

Hasseif El Sharif
Wandering Star Master of the Dawn

While I was writing the last three paragraphs, my pen ran out of ink. The final two paragraphs can only be read by the strong impression of pen upon paper, and in the morning, the pen worked fine again.

And then I beheld a simple vision

Which imprinted into my being,

Soaring swiftly to my soul

A sight which could never be forgotten . . . .

I beheld a flock of small white birds

Flying together in the formation

Of one vast, radiant white Birdstar. . . .

Then the doors to Remembrance

Flung fully open . . . .

Archangel Uriel Speaks:

I am Archangel Uriel, Overseer of Above. My realms are the Celestial Vastness. Within my starry Heavens, the Seventh Star has been birthed under my watchful protection. I monitored the three triangular baffles that they remained in constant positional alignment to create the resonant field for the Seventh Star's glorious moment of birth. Always have I been like a proud and responsible parent, guiding the creations within my sphere with the wisdom of Love. Constantly observing with joyous wonder, the continued expansion of Divine Purpose as it manifests both on Heaven and Earth.

After the Seventh Star was born, I Called forth the Birdstar to emerge from the heart of the Seventh Star. And I have also Called forth the Birdstar to emerge from the depths of your loving hearts. My first Call to you announcing the return of the Birdstar was issued in late 1988. There have since been two more Calls. This is the time to heed my Call and birth the Birdstar from within your hearts, then to take your position within its shining body.

What is the significance of this vast white bird, you might ask? And rightly so, for you must know. This radiant, shimmering, almost transparent Birdstar is you, me, all the Heavenly Hosts and humanity combined. It is our Homeward Vehicle created by uniting as One. It is a large fragment of our Star now embarking on its Homeward Journey. It is the vehicle for our mass ascension. And we shall not be leaving the planet Earth behind, for she shall travel within the heart of our vast Body of Light.

The moment now approaches when the Doorway shall open and our magnificent Birdstar will arise in fullest flight, filling the entire Heavens. Together as One, we will travel through this Doorway into the Greater Reality. This journey will take twenty years as measured in earthly time, for such is the vastness of our Heavenly Birdstar.

I have Called you to awaken and remember, to birth the Birdstar within your hearts, and to rise up into the fullness of your Angelic Presence that you may take your preordained position within the massive body of our great, white bird. That we may truly fly as One.

And it matters not if you find yourself in the beak or tail, as tip of wing or snuggled deep within its belly. For each of you is needed for our Birdstar to fly. Each of us is necessary to create the whole. You are more important to the fulfillment of the Divine Plan than you can presently imagine.

Together we are the Birdstar. Together we shall fly into our glorious future as One. Together we will make the long awaited Homeward Journey. Thus have we entered the magnificent Time of Completion.

The Birdstar Returns

Long ago, we were encoded with our pre-ordained star patternings in the shape of a Birdstar / Starbird.

The present activation of this image of the Birdstar symbolizes that we are entering our Time of Completion from our long immersion into duality. This shall free us from the entire dimensional cycle of experience to move onward into a New Octave of Oneness.

As has been stated, the Birdstar is our Homeward Vehicle. But in order that there be no confusion, we shall say again that *the Birdstar is not a spaceship.* It has merely been perceived that way by those with a more limited perception of the Higher Truths. Spaceships or starships merely are concentrations or emanations of Light and energy frequency pulsations.

I, too, have visited aboard various spaceships, been well treated, taken on thorough tours of the facilities. Yet, each time I am strongly told that the form is merely an illusion! The reason why we sometimes perceive them in this manner is due to our remaining ties to matter. So if you are one of the ones sitting around waiting for the big spaceship in the sky to land and take you off planet Earth, you might have a long wait. Sure, something might land and offer you a ride, but it might not take you to where you really want to go, which is Home—back to the One.

The Birdstar is manifested by our focused intent and the purity of our Love. When we speak of its *return,* we refer to the return of its Essence which has always resided within us as unmanifest potential. It is up to us to quicken it with life, by our willingness to surrender into the Greater Reality, by our loving commitment to become One, and by our deep yearnings to return to the state of consciousness called Home.

The Birdstar's return signifies a new phase of heightened awareness when we begin to regard ourselves, first, as planetary citizens, then as interplanetary citizens, leading to the realization of what is termed the All That Is.

Already, this great awakening can be felt resounding throughout this planet as humanity cries out for freedom and unity. There is a new global awareness of Gaia, our sweet Earth, as one, interrelated, interdependent sphere of consciousness.

All of this prepares us to rise up and take our pre-ordained positions within the vast body of our beautiful Birdstar. The time of our victorious ascension into Oneness has begun. We join together as one vast, starry Legion of Light, melded into a drop of purest Essence.

Together as One, we shall rise up from the dissolving illusions of duality and fly. On our ascension journey, we shall pass through the gateway of No-Time for therein resides the Greater Reality which we have long sought in the depths of our beings.

In our eternal union with the One, we will find abiding fulfillment and Love beyond measure.

We fly suspended,
gliding gently upward.
The jewel in the center,
that reflection of our true nature,
beckons to us, leads us on, lights our way –
a beacon in the starry eye of God,
our hearts can only follow.
Waves of Light turn in upon themselves
& merge into One Heart.
The instant of surrender will find each
in their position of Light.
Nothing more to be done, only letting go.
Zero in on that shining Golden Star
& let it lead you Home.

. . . . Solasia

Pure Drop

Beloved Star-Borne Ones,
you who have been birthed from the stars
and who shall return to the stars –
you who are a star,
this journey of remembrance & reawakening
is almost complete.
The veils of forgetfulness have been lifted.
Your long slumber is over.
Never again, shall you forget
that which you truly are.
Never again, will you feel separate
from the One.

For now you know who you are
and your magnificent Angelic Presence
has anchored deeply within your being.
The Golden Solar Angels of the Great Central Sun
have hereby been reactivated
in order to serve their chosen destiny
upon planet Earth and Beyond.

And you have heard the Call to Return
issued forth across the starry Heavens.
It has resounded throughout your molecules,
echoing all the way into heart's sacred central core.

You know that the Time of Completion is here,
And you are joyously ready and fully prepared
to rise into the New Octave of the Greater Reality.
With wisdom, love and empowerment,
you take your position within the Light Body
of the radiant Birdstar which Calls us Homeward.

Together we are already One.
We have always been united as One.
And it is with utmost Love and Respect
that we honor the all-pervading Oneness
of our Greater Reality.

Beloved Ones, you who have traveled so far,
now your journey returns you Home to the Star . . . .

I Am Solaris Antari:

The time has come, my beloved ones, to stand up and step forward into the fullness of that which you truly are.

The Call has sounded. The doorway doth open wide. You have heard the Celestial Song resonate within the inner sanctum of your heart.

Do you yet have doubts? They are merely the dust of illusion. Shake them gently away and experience the freedom you have long sought. It beckons you to embrace it fully and to surrender. For surrendering is the key. The key to be.

And although it be said that there is choice; in truth, there is no choice but surrender. It's simply easier to do it with love and laughter, to do it with trust and openness.

For the Winds of Change doth blow us into the Unknown. And there you are sent to expand and grow. The Unknown can only be explored in a state of complete surrender for it is totally different than anything you have previously experienced. There you shall find all that you seek. Your yearnings and your love shall draw to you all that your heart has called for.

The Crystal Call is sent forth and finds response. For indeed, many are being called forth to gather together. The fragments of star doth reunite.

And the Winds of Change shall scatter these seeds far and wide, yet separate them not. For all the seeds are of the One. In the core, they are the same. Once this is known and experienced, it shall never be forgotten. The more we remember, we are increasingly linked by shared Essence. We are truly One. Our radiant, shining Star which illuminates with purest Love, shall grow ever brighter as each of us remembers.

Unfurl your wings as you surrender to the wind, fly where you may for you are needed everywhere. Each of you is an open doorway. Each of you is a shining Pillar of Light, a beacon for many others, illuminating the passage through the doorway into the realms of Celestial Vastness which leads homeward. This is the reunion of the Star That We Are!

Inside the Gate of Heaven is where we are right now. We have merely to remember. By our seeing of the Unseen, by our listening to the fullness of Silence, by our receiving the Higher Frequencies emanating from On High, we begin to embody that which originates from the realms of Heaven, that which is Divine.

We are the harbingers of Heaven, the messengers of the Dawn. The New Morning is upon us!

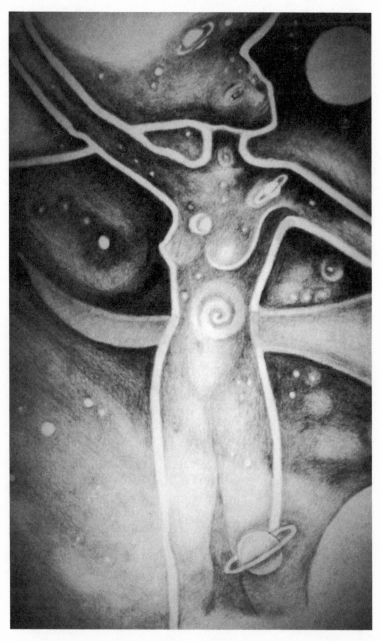

"Universe Within" by Sheoekah Amu (Mary St. Marie).

Each of us who has touched the stars
Becomes a lantern which illuminates
All with starry Light.

Wherever we go, whatever we do,
We bring with us myriad Golden Stars –
Stars which transform!

We are the transformers,
 Sent into realms where previously
Even Angels did not dare to tread.
Yet, now we go everywhere
Until nothing remains untouched by us.
Everything is imbedded with tiny Golden Stars.
Our calling cards – the Starseeds of
Transformation.

As we travel bringing change,
We become the most profoundly changed.
Touched ever deeper by the stars
Until we metamorphose into stars ourselves.

Acknowledgements:

There are always special beings who serve us as touchstones, reminding us who we are, encouraging us, bringing clarity into confusion, giving us strength and healing when most needed, being willing to listen and understand.

Many gifts have I received for which I am most grateful—be they gifts of love, the sharing of tears, patience, wisdom, financial support, music, labor or laughter. All of these have kept me going when I felt too weary to continue.

Although there has been a constant fluctuation of people in my life and many of those mentioned here have since gone their seemingly separate ways, I lovingly thank all of you who have lightened my journey, especially:

Nova & Nion Sheppard: my two youngest children and special starry souls—who have generously tolerated an unusual mother who spends much time writing and traveling, instead of baking cookies.

Elara Zacandra: my eldest daughter—who is wise beyond her knowing.

Sola: my beloved cat—who will never read this book, yet understands it all.
Lázaro Ama-Ra: for helping me when it was most needed.
Solasia: for helping birth the Seventh Star.
Grace (Lumiere Amurai): for her depth of soul.
Marion Starnes: for being a beacon of Light during my emergence.
Doris Hartshorn (Helios Corona): who always had the patience to listen & the depth to understand.

Matisha my Angel brother, Elariul, Anyara, Chanondeley, Mimi Kamp—for her drawings & flower essences, Elisabeth Kubler Ross (Kumara), Staravia Christus, Richard Leviton, Alonssi & Blaise, Dee Dee & Bill, Elonai, Tom Eiden, Gary Applegate, Bryce Bond (Solnama), Natazuel–for journeying with me to the Beyond, Sujak, Marie St. Marie, Lee Driver, Alairius, Solamé, Aman-Anca, Master Ni, Hua Ching–for teaching me about Shiens, Taner Celensu–for my awakening, Laolyn–for my birth, Aqliaqua & Ramariel for their enduring Love and support, and all the rest of our magnificent Starry Family worldwide!

I would like to pay homage to some whom I have never met, but would be honored to:

Doris Lessing – Master Writer, whose book, *The Marriage Between Zones Three, Four & Five* always triggers deep remembrance.

Vangelis – Master Musician of Atlantis & Beyond, who evokes with full authority the power & majesty of the Celestial Realms.

Stephen Hawking – Astrophysicist, black holes made simple, for bringing physics closer to metaphysics.

Ken Carey –Fellow traveler from the stars.

And most especially to the owners of New Age Bookstores everywhere, who serve us all by anchoring the Light!

Solara Antara Amaa-Ra . . . .

I am simply an open doorway.
Once this doorway has been discovered
And safely passed through by others,
I am free to find hitherto Unknown doorways.

I reside in the Great Silence of Beyond the Beyond.
My true form is the starry vastness of merged Essence.
I am found within all of you, as you are within me.
Together as One, we are returning Home to the Star . . . .

Other Books by Solara

how to LIVE LARGE on a small planet $15.95

  How to anchor our vastness into our physical bodies
  and become Vibrantly Alive!

11:11 – *Inside the Doorway* $15.95

  A visionary revelation of the 11:11 Cosmology.

EL*AN*RA – *The Healing of Orion*

  A wild love story set in the stars containing
  the keys to free you from duality! $14.95

The Star-Borne:
  A Remembrance for the Awakened Ones

  A vast Handbook of Remembrance! $14.95

The Legend of Altazar

  A profoundly moving story of Atlantis, Lemuria &
  AN to unify your head and heart. $12.95

Invoking Your Celestial Guardians

  How to contact & embody your Golden Solar Angel.
                                              $10.00

Star-Borne Unlimited
6477 Hwy 93 South #6511
Whitefish, Montana 59937 USA

US Funds only on a US Check or money order. Please include $4.00 shipping
for first item .50¢ for each additional item. *(Overseas shipping extra.)*

Audio Cassettes by Solara
with music by Etherium

The Starry Council $10.00 each
Temple Invisible
True Love/One Heart
Unifying the Polarities
Voyage on the Celestial Barge
Archangel Mikael Empowerment
Star Alignments
Remembering Your Story
The Star That We Are
The Angel You Truly Are

Musical Journeys

The Lotus of True Love
Through the Doorway

Sacred Dance Series *by Etherium & Omashar*

The Earth-Star Dance
The Sacred Spiral Dance
The Greater Central Sun Dance
The Starry Processional

Starry Songs Live!

The Tahitian Star-Borne Reunion
Second Gate in Ecuador
The Australian Star-Borne Reunion